Living and Working
in Other Cultures

Dealing with the Dutch

Living and Working
in Other Cultures

DEALING
WITH THE DUTCH

Jacob Vossestein

ROYAL TROPICAL INSTITUTE

© 1997 ROYAL TROPICAL INSTITUTE (KIT) - AMSTERDAM

Second edition, 1998

Third edition, 1998

Cover and design: Peter Vermeulen, Ontwerpbureau Amsterdam, Amsterdam

Photographs cover: Paul Romein, Fotobureau KIT

Drawings: Franka van der Loo

Lay-out: Basislijn, Henny Scholten

Printing: Drukkerij Haasbeek BV, Alphen aan den Rijn

ISBN 90-6832-557-4

NUGI 684

The books which are published in the series *Living and Working in Other Cultures* are based on briefings and training programmes given by the CMD Department (Culture, Management and Development) of the Royal Tropical Institute (KIT). Over the years the CMD Department has gained intercultural knowledge and experience within an international environment. KIT has been investigating the characteristics of cultures for almost a century. KIT staff members are able to identify with employees of other organisations: the international business community, international donor organisations, governments in developing countries, and other organisations which post expatriates abroad.

In recent years CMD has expanded its training programme on country-oriented information and business briefings with courses on Western and Eastern European countries as well as the United States. The book *Dealing with the Dutch* is based on the course 'Understanding the Dutch'.

The series *Living and Working in Other Cultures* is the continuation of the series *Living and Working in the Tropics*. The following issues have been published:

P.A. Slors, *Huispersoneel, raakvlak met andere culturen*, 1987 (sold out)

P.R. Voogt, *Onderhandelen in Zuidoost-Azië*, 1992.

E. Kunst, M. Simons en F. Öry, *Opgroeien in het buitenland*, 1993.

C. Ukpabi, *Doing business in Africa*, 1995.

E. Kunst, M. Simons en H. Zorn, *Terug in Nederland*, 1996.

I. Groenen, *Vanuit de partner gezien*, 1997.

Jacob Vossestein (1949, Utrecht, the Netherlands) studied human geography and social anthropology and has travelled widely. As a KIT staff member since 1979, he has developed 'country briefings' for Dutch expatriates-to-be. Since 1988 he has also been responsible for KIT's 'Understanding the Dutch' training programmes for foreign expatriates living in the Netherlands. These are given some 25 times per year for multinational companies including Shell, Unilever, ABN/Amro Bank, DSM, Eastman Chemicals and TNT Worldwide Express.

CONTENTS

FOREWORD

This book is meant for readers from other countries who have dealings with the Netherlands through work or business.

Foreigners working with Dutch people seldom experience problems related to sloth or inefficiency. If their work brings them to Holland itself, it is rarely inadequate infrastructure that bothers them, or other problems involving logistics and 'hardware'. Expatriates residing in the Netherlands hardly ever suffer from inadequate housing, insecurity or lack of facilities for the accompanying family. Few people have to worry about such aspects, after the phase of settling in, which always produces some uneasiness.

Rather, they keep telling me it is the underlying values and norms of their Dutch colleagues (or counterparts, or subordinates) that puzzle them and sometimes cause irritation.

What this book intends to do, therefore, is to focus on this system of values and norms. Using quotations from foreigners who have already dealt with the Dutch, I shall put these observations into the wider context of Dutch culture and society. I shall concentrate on the level of everyday contacts in work and business, informing you about what is likely to happen in Holland and advising you on how to overcome misunderstandings and prevent irritation.

Norms and values are not stable, but in recent years, Dutch society has been changing rather rapidly. Old structures like religion, ideologies and family life seem to be breaking up, while 'the hot breath of the market' has now, after affecting Dutch companies, also touched government policies. The younger generations have a different, at times even sharply contrasting, view of life and the world than their elders. However, cultural characteristics and 'typical behaviour' do not change overnight. They may re-appear in other forms. I have tried to take this into account by, on the one hand, sketching present-day Dutch culture with its underlying, historical roots, while on the other, embellishing the picture with examples of changes that appear crucial.

One widespread misunderstanding should be cleared up. So far, the names 'Holland' and 'the Netherlands' have been used as if they are identical, just two names for the same country. In English, this is more or less correct, although the more official term 'the Netherlands' is preferred for ceremonial or diplomatic purposes.[1] However, the Dutch among themselves use the word 'Holland' specifically to indicate the most important and dominant area of the country: the highly urbanized western provinces of Noord- and Zuid-Holland plus Utrecht, the so-called Randstad (see map). This ring of cities is the economic, cultural and political heart of the nation.

In most cases Dutch business encounters will take place there, and you will then be dealing with 'Hollanders', people originating there or at least living there now. Since this 'Holland proper' exercises strong influences elsewhere through national institutions and the media, this book deals mostly with the mentality of that area. Only if differences to other areas are really striking will I become more explicit. More information on other areas will be given in chapter 9.

Thus, the following chapters focus on what one might call the average behaviour of the ethnic Dutch majority, in the field of business and work. But like other European countries, the Netherlands is fast turning into a multicultural society. Including Dutch citizens from former colonies, more than a million people with slightly or strongly different cultures have moved to Holland in recent decades. Although assimilation and acculturation do take place, many of them (still) show behaviour that is not totally in line with the mentality described in this book. More on the ethnic minorities and immigrant cultures can be found in chapter 10.

Generalization is virtually inevitable in a book like this. Even when discussing the mainstream culture, nuances should be kept in mind all the time. A nation's culture is never homogeneous. Even in the smallest country there are differences in values, views and manners between various groups of the population, between generations, etc. Some of these issues related to gender and generations are discussed in chapter 8.

As for the business world, another factor is important enough to mention here. The Dutch economy being open and internationally oriented, many Dutch business people have been changed by wide exposure to foreign cultures. At least in their working life, and possibly in their private life as well, their manners may no longer be 'typically Dutch', but the result of a kind of international culture. Obviously, to foreign business people such Dutchmen are 'easier' to deal with. Since these internationally experienced people are in a minority, this book tries to prepare you for a more likely situation: dealing mainly with people who do not have this international outlook, who behave in 'typically' Dutch ways. They may be found in smaller companies only now exploring cross-border markets, but also in larger and/or multinational companies, where not everyone at all levels is exposed to the outside world.

Whatever your particular situation, I hope to be able to clarify certain characteristic types of Dutch behaviour that you are likely to encounter sooner or later.

What then are these characteristics? After years of training foreign business people and other professionals in the field of Dutch culture, I have amalgamated the following essentials, which form the basis for the chapters that follow:

- egalitarian
- direct and critical
- pragmatic and money-minded
- strong on procedures and yet permissive
- tolerant or indifferent?
- the international outlook.

Throughout the book I will quote observations by foreigners residing in the Netherlands, most of them for work reasons. The quotations were collected personally from interviews in Dutch newspapers or magazines, or verbally communicated to me by participants of the training programmes called 'Understanding the Dutch', which have been organised by the Royal Tropical Institute several times a year since 1989. I regret the fact that besides their nationality, more detail on the people quoted is usually lacking.

Jacob Vossestein

1. Compare 'Great Britain' (or 'The United Kingdom') and 'England'.

THE NETHERLANDS

- ● City >100.000 inh.
- ● Other important towns: (not shown in Randstad area)
- Randstad (5 million inh.)
- <u>Assen</u> Provincial capital
- Provincial boundaries
- Rivers and canals
- Area less than 1 meter (3,3 ft.) above sealevel: without protection or dikes or dunes, this would be flooded
- Dams and barriers (Delta and Zuiderzee projects)

Chapter 1

ON IMAGES AND STEREOTYPES

'Ah, you're from Holland? Such a nice little country,
with flowers everywhere. Pity it always rains there.'
(French lady talking to the author in a train
from Paris to Nice.)

Everyone coming into contact with people from another country has some preconceived ideas about that country. In the modern world such pictures are mostly created by the media. Even the remotest country inspires some mental picture of what it might be like, however vague or stereotypical. Of course, stereotypes are not representative of the whole picture, but they are often also not totally without some truth. They usually reflect a certain characteristic, possibly out of context, stripped of its real meaning and function. Yet the stereotype is what most people start from; it colours their expectations and their initial perception. Only when working among or with the people to whom the stereotype refers does one learn about the context, the nuances, the validity of the generalisation. The same of course applies to the stereotypes about Holland.

The Netherlands is not exactly a remote country, being in the heart of Europe, nor is it absent from the international media. In other words, there are several images of Holland, some truer than others, some suggested by Dutch institutions, some definitely not.

The images prevalent abroad differ widely. They depend on the observer's national origins because the way someone perceives a foreign country always involves that person's own cultural background.

This can be clearly seen in the quotations reproduced in this book, which besides commenting on the Dutch usually also reveal something of the observer's own frame of reference. For example, the above quotation from the French lady says something of France, too, its size, its climate, the apparent lack of flowers in her home town. It also reflects the observer's social position and the sources from which (s)he acquired the information. It makes quite a difference whether one reads (certain) newspapers, or has worked with Dutch people, or made several short business visits to the Netherlands, or had contact in any other way.

Be that as it may, let us try and make an inventory of the most important images of Holland that surface in foreign publications.

The sturdy image: a low and wet country with neverending rain, most of it lying below sea level, sure to be flooded if it were not for the windmills, the famous Delta Works and little Hans Brinker stopping the leakages in the dyke with his index finger.

The tourist image (the French lady's): a mostly agrarian idyll, charming Queen Beatrix ruling an innocent little country, its inhabitants peacefully producing milk and cheese, vegetables, flowers and flower bulbs, while living (if not in windmills) in quaintly gabled old houses, wearing wooden shoes and riding bicycles.

The economic image (promoted by Dutch business): the Gateway to Europe, a successful trading nation, home to internationally operating companies like Royal Dutch Shell, Unilever, Philips, Heineken, KLM, Akzo-Nobel, Ahold, DSM and ABN/Amro Bank. Strategically operating ones also, as shown by ING Bank buying Barings Bank from Great Britain and its dairy industries supplying half the globe with cheese and milk powder. Competitive, too, with a stable social climate, a well-educated workforce, a favourable tax situation: the 'polder model': suddenly since 1996 this name has popped up to describe the Dutch economic miracle resulting in job creation, stable and internationally competitive wage levels and – for European standards – booming economic growth figures. It is seen as a successful model for restructuring the European welfare states into more flexible economies without breaking down their social benefit system. Foreign delegations and the press come to study the mysterious kind of harmony between Dutch employers and trade unions, in which the government keeps a very low profile. At the G7 Conference in Denver in July 1997, US President Clinton invited the Dutch Prime Minister (he was attending because the Netherlands was EU president at the time) to explain this model to the other leaders present.

This image is in rather stark contrast to what might be described as the 'lenient image'. Until quite recently, international organizations like the OECD and the World Bank had been criticizing the Netherlands for its luxurious system of social benefits based on extremely high taxes, which was ruining the nation's economic position.

The tight-with-money image (popular in neighbouring countries): a money-minded nation whose greatest pleasure is scraping money out of every transaction. When on vacation, Dutch people drag their own potatoes in caravans through Europe rather than spend their money in local restaurants.

The permissive image (held up by foreign journalists): a far too liberal society, where specialised shops sell legal drugs and pornography to people indulging in nudism, who find it perfectly normal that gay couples (married in the town hall, of course) obtain children through artificial insemination, and where people are helped to their death by wandering doctors who legally practise euthanasia.

The self-conceited image (hinted at in diplomatic circles): a tiny country with a big mouth, wanting to seem larger than it is, its people tactlessly expressing their opinions on other people's affairs.

The sportive image: a nation of good soccer/football players, unfortunately accompanied by hooligans violently expressing their anti-German sentiments.

Stereotypes usually hold a grain of truth. Over-generalising and contradictory as the images may be, many Dutchmen will recognise them. Sometimes they agree with them, although they will probably not let them pass without comment (which, of course, nicely fits in with their image of always knowing better than everyone else).

Some of these stereotypes could be seen as contradictory, for example: How can such 'money minded' people accept those heavy taxes? How can pornography be associated with wooden shoe wearing flower growers? Where do the nice old gables fit in with the 'legal' drugs? How can an industrial nation successfully compete on an image of cheese and windmills? Why are these football hooligans so anti-German, being born about 30 years after the Second World War?

These contradictions and the wide scope of the stereotypes reflect a pluriform society accommodating a broad variety of lifestyles and views within a very small surface area. Condensing them, a picture emerges of a country that does not avoid challenges but is willing to try solutions that may be out of the ordinary.

This sounds rather fascinating and provocative, and it could easily evoke the idea that the Netherlands is a land of non-conformists. There certainly are such people around, and Dutch television happily presents them to an eager audience, yet most foreigners experience something quite different: a highly organised country of great regularity, where public transport works with admirable precision, where rules written and unwritten are respected, where, in spite of all the permissiveness, most people seem to follow a set pattern of daily activities. As an illustration, a Spanish lady working in Holland for some time exclaimed: *'Sometimes I wonder if the Dutch have blood in their veins, or milk!'*

This picture is quite contrary to the one painted before: conformity rather than unconventionality, boring rather than fascinating. The Spanish comment reveals something of the despair a person from a more emotional, warm-blooded culture may experience in Holland.

And yet there are those sex shops, those social experiments and daring laws with unusual solutions, those stubborn Dutchmen who will go their own way in spite of conventions. More paradoxes, in other words.

Chapter 2

ON EGALITARIANISM AND AUTHORITY

'Geen kapsones!'
(Dutch slang expression, rebuking 'airs', arrogance)

As Western Europe is busy endlessly discussing its attempts at unification and the rest of the continent is insecure about its future, all over Europe terms like 'nation', 'culture', 'ethnicity' and 'identity' are heard. The Dutch have been protagonists of European unity ever since 1945, and not just because their trade economy thrives on open borders. But now that unification is really dawning, doubts are setting in. Should the Queen step down, what about Parliament, the flag, the Dutch guilder? Will the cultural and social achievements of a smaller country be safe-guarded? Can the Dutch language, institutions and identity survive in the long run?

In recent discussions on the question of what exactly is Dutch identity, what sets the Dutch apart from other nations, various journalists and philosophers arrived at the conclusion that at the heart of Dutch culture lies 'egalitarianism', a sense of everyone being equal from a moral point of view. As an essential value, this is not easy to see right away, it lies hidden in Dutch behaviour and institutions. Foreigners may need some time to start grasping its importance. What they notice at first is a certain lack of decorum, that quite a few Dutchmen ignore hierarchy or status, the do-it-yourself aspect of society. Depending, of course, also on their own backgrounds, they comment on a lack of service orientation in the Netherlands, but also on the approachability of the authorities. They sense a lack of appreciation for outstanding performance, or a certain uniformity in Dutch (modern) housing, and a surprising degree of workers' participation in companies.

More examples will be given later, but all these things can only be explained by taking into account this Dutch egalitarianism. It is deeply rooted in history and, according to some observers, even in the flat scenery. It has quite a few consequences for people's everyday behaviour, both inside and outside the business world. Even conduct apparently quite contradictory to egalitarianism is often, consciously or not, nothing but a dissociation from this core value.

Let us see how one foreigner perceives it: *'If anyone here sticks out from the crowd, his head is chopped off. There is always criticism. They always tear people down, good performance is played down. Everyone must be the same, there shouldn't be anyone brilliant.'* (Argentine)

'Just act normal, that is strange enough' Maybe this often used Dutch expression says it all. It is informally given as an ironic comment when someone's behaviour or opinions are perceived as exceptional, overdone. It is a call for conventionality: blend in with the others, conform, do not stick out.

This may come as a surprise in a country that also has a reputation for permissiveness, for liberal attitudes towards non-conformist lifestyles, and legal rights for all sorts of minority views and behaviour.

Upon closer inspection, one might discover that the call for equality, for conformity, relates not so much to the behaviour or opinion itself, but to the moral stance that people attach to it. It tells them they may be very special indeed but that this should not make them feel or behave superior to others. The message is: be or think whatever you want, but don't boast of it, and don't expect any privilege or more respect than anyone else.

Therefore, material extravagancies and high profile behaviour are not appreciated. Anyone with authority or with exceptional talents should subtly show that although (s)he may have power, money or prestige, nevertheless (s)he is modest, approachable, democratic.

Academic titles In Dutch society, the use of titles should be limited to the functional working environment. Using them in private life does occasionally occur, but most people find this boastful rather than respectful. If titles are not backed up by reality (as frequently happens in some countries), their use is a social disgrace, as one well-known Dutchmen found out. He decided to disappear abroad to obtain his degree after all.

Although excellent performers in the fields of arts, sports and business are certainly applauded in Holland, they should remain 'humane' and accessible to everyone. They should present themselves with some modesty, appreciate their fellow competitors, share their glory with others. Anyone lending assistance or support should be included in their victory, mentioned by name, hauled up onto the platform with the winner. If they don't, terms like 'swaggering' and 'arrogance' pop up quickly. One example of this involved the disapproving letters in newspapers when, after the completion of an enormous bridge across a river, only government people, engineers and other 'big shots' were invited to the official opening, and not the many construction workers that finished the complicated job before the deadline. The organisers should have known better.

A very clever man   A recent letter to the editor of Holland's leading intellectual newspaper referred to an interview with a person who was in charge of the World Jamboree, a massive international gathering of scouts, held in the Netherlands in 1995: 'While reading [that interview] I thought: how clever this man could do all that by himself, and how important he must be, chatting and meeting with the Queen and the State Secretary of Sports. As a coach [of the participants] I observed however that the success of most activities depended rather on the collaborators at the workfloor. (...) Nothing in the interview shows this man's appreciation for and his dependence on these thousands of volunteers. It was only by these volunteers' inventivity and creativity that things threatening to go wrong (...) were dealt with in a pleasant and efficient way.'

No airs please   The basic idea of the equality issue is that everyone merely uses their God-given talents. It is sheer luck to have them, nothing more. In the past God was to be thanked for them, nowadays it may be nature, DNA, good trainers, anything but not strictly personal excellence. According to this view, in essence no one is really any better than anyone else. Success should not go to one's head. The successful and famous should still wait for their turn and apologise or only humbly accept if others give them privileges. They should not spend their entire fortune on selfish pleasures but have others share in it to some degree.

Although in recent years more public pride of one's individual performance is allowed, low profile and accessibility are still widely appreciated. No airs please, down to earth in a flat country.

Having said this, we should remember that egalitarianism is a virtue, that is, appreciated and desired behaviour. It does not mean that each and every Dutchman lives according to this. But if they don't, they may expect criticism. The Dutch language has some 20 words for boasting and swaggering!

Authorities like ministers and politicians should (and do) keep in mind that power games and glorious status symbols may be useful in foreign contacts of an official nature, but once they have returned home, they'd better climb down from their pedestals and avoid ivory towers regarding dress, language, the use of chauffeurs (only for work please!) and in many more ways. Only during foreign contacts may the State Secretary of Economic Affairs call herself the Minister of Trade. Authority figures including members of the royal family have been fined by the police for breaking traffic regulations, and this deeply satisfied the nation: just like us, not any better. Act normal.

Egalitarianism and the business world   In the business world, the effect of all this is that Dutch directors and general managers are quite aware of the limits this egalitarianism sets on their exercise of authority. Since their staff and personnel are usually well educated and aware of their importance for the company, they demand, and have, a say in affairs. They speak up when things aren't to their liking, not only concerning the whereabouts of the coffee machine but also in far more decisive matters. Such equal rights and respect for all levels of the workplace are reflected in the phenomenon of the company council, quite normal in Europe but not as much in other countries: *'I admire your law on company councils. To American standards it is unbelievable that (..) a representative organ of workers can criticise the management and stop certain decisions.'* (USA)

In the Netherlands, every company with more than 35 workers is legally required to have a workers' council (called O.R. in its Dutch abbreviation).[1] This system of company democracy generally functions quite well under normal circumstances. Participants are elected by their fellow-workers, and the employer is obliged to allow them to be trained for their council activities during working hours. Trade unions may play a role in the background but are not intimately involved.

At the department level there are what the Dutch call literally 'work-discussions' (werkoverleg) and 'functioning-talks' (functionerings-gesprekken), in which lower and higher levels are supposed to mutually vent their opinions on each other's performance, general behaviour and attitudes.

The result is that in most Dutch companies and institutions there is a constant flow of information on policy, planning, procedures, results, and not only from the top to the bottom.

This is not to everyone's liking, because it can be distracting from everyday chores, and of course there is also criticism on the quality, legibility and length of all these papers or meetings.

When the going gets rough, Dutch managers and bosses cannot easily make a fist and say: '*I'm the boss, this is what I want and all of you must do so!*' The employees would fiercely protest such coercion and possibly sabotage this 'authoritarianism'. If the situation does escalate, many companies and organisations in Holland, more so than in other countries, involve external trouble shooters and *interim* managers to solve conflicts and suggest restructuring. Outsiders can more successfully implement unwelcome changes than people from inside, no matter what their position.

If outsiders are not wanted, it may be sufficiently effective for the management to explain the difficult situation seriously to the workers and ask for their cooperation in solving it. Attempts will be made to soften unpleasant but necessary measures, like shorter work hours for everyone rather than dismissing people, or (if this is inevitable) 'natural discharge', that is: a stop on taking on new personnel, early retirement for older or sick workers, outplacement facilities for people leaving voluntarily, and 'golden handshakes' for the more highly placed individuals.

Dismissing people is not easy in the Netherlands. Dutch law as a whole reflects the country's egalitarian values. Dutch labour legislation strongly supports employees in their legal rights and protects people in vulnerable positions from injustice and arbitrariness. Only in a few specific cases (openhanded theft and the like) may employees be sacked right away. In any less simple labour conflict, workers will fight their dismissal in court (backed up by free legal assistance and/or trade union support), because if they don't, their rights to social security will not be recognised. Since the employee is almost automatically considered 'the weaker party', judges will often give them the advantage, by prohibiting dismissal or by granting them some kind of bonus.

As a result of all this 'protecting the weak', the labour market in the Netherlands cannot be called 'flexible', when compared with the USA and the Asian 'Tigers'. (Compared with many other West European countries, this situation is not all that bad.) Some foreigners working in Holland have trouble understanding the system. In 1993 a Turkish manager observed: *'A higher labour participation, more flexible hire-and-fire procedures, fewer taxes and therefore lower cost of labour would benefit prosperity: higher production, more people at work and more income to distribute. Isn't that much more righteous than distributing work and income among a small, privileged group while putting the others off with social benefits?'*

Recent changes Exactly this kind of change has been worked on intensively for the past 10 years. In the face of increasing international competition and in line with general European labour regulations, Dutch companies are promoting a more flexible labour market. Since dismissals are complicated and lengthy procedures, companies are becoming increasingly careful in hiring people on a permanent basis. The slim-line organisation is therefore a popular concept in the Netherlands, resulting in a high degree of automation and computerisation rather than a large number of staff members. Temporary workers are brought in to bridge any peak periods. Hired through temp agencies, they can be dismissed with far more flexibility. The proportion of temporary workers in Holland is one of the highest in the world, since the associated side-effect of part-time work is also popular (see chapter 8). It is one of the pillars of the polder model.

Recent government policy supports all this, to some degree, but it is not an easy task, because the present system gives many people the satisfaction of righteousness and safety. Only the younger generation of professionals seems willing or even eager to take a chance and play the game. The older generation of workers and the less educated segments of the labour market have a hard time with it. They protest politically either by voting for other parties or by opposing 'Europe'. Some go looking for shelter in quieter niches of the labour market.

Dutch labour legislation is gradually changing, as younger generations with a different value system move up in the business world. Flexible work schedules and large differences in salary are increasingly being considered normal and accepted.

Egalitarianism plays another role in everyday working life, in the field of personal relations. Employees in lower positions should definitely not be treated as 'subordinates', as inferiors who only carry out the boss's orders. Dutch workers are (usually) responsible and hardworking. They like to work independently on their task without being checked all the time. Since in most cases the boss may count on them, he or she should consult them rather than order them around. By being open and approachable, superiors make not only themselves more acceptable but also the hierarchy which is unavoidable but slightly embarrassing to the Dutch. Superiors with this management style, 'human', friendly, not merely 'using' their personnel functionally, may count on loyal cooperation, even when the circumstances demand speed, over-time and stress.

Secretaries   When dealing with a Dutch secretary, it is advisable to keep a low profile as well, and not be 'bossy'. A good working relation requires mutual trust in capacities and responsibilities, concern about each others' working methods and workload. Your Dutch secretary prefers to be your efficient window to the company and the outside world, rather than a mere executor of chores or a trouble shooter. Some openness about your family affairs and private interests is important also, and will be reciprocated. It indicates that, whether boss or secretary, both are also just people.

'Higher people' and arrogance   All this does not imply that there aren't any 'higher' people, that there is no elite, that there are no authorities in the Netherlands. Of course, there are, and they are recognisable to the general public by their appearance, speech, expensive cars and houses, etc. But in Holland such status is less taken for granted than in other countries. Wealth and power are something to be modest about, because to the Dutch they should be backed up by high moral standards.

Whenever a flaw is detected in the fulfilment of the high expectations that authority or excellence encourage, the criticism starts. In Dutch culture, being rich and mighty is not enough to gain public prestige. Any sign of high profile or pride may easily be interpreted as 'arrogance'. The good aspects will then be overlooked, and the weaker ones fully exposed in private discussion or in the press. This has happened to captains of industry, but also to actors, politicians, artists, and even to royalty.

It takes a long time for these people to overcome such criticism, because any new accomplishment will be scrutinized for repetitions of the disapproved behaviour or attitude. Obviously, a low profile is advisable, both in times of success and afterwards.

For successful people (also from the business world), it is easier to live away from the continuous scrutiny of the Dutch press and public. Another reason may well be that foreign taxes are lower, but some well-known authors, successful painters and actors who moved abroad sourly commented that to them 'Holland is too small, too narrow-minded'. Famous soccer players, for example, accepted Italian and other foreign contracts, certainly also because excellence is more highly rewarded there, in terms of finance and privilege. And last but not least, upon retiring, many Dutch long-term expatriates prefer to settle down in other countries than return home. The climate may be one reason, but certainly not the only one: after years of living in societies with more allowance for privilege and luxury, readjusting to Dutch society is not easy.

The Dutch may regret this and criticise it, but they will not change their own basic attitude. It is too deeply engrained in the culture.

Regarding taxes and salaries, Dutch salary scales and the tax system also reflect the drive for equality. Just a few years ago research revealed that Dutch managers and directors earn quite a bit less than comparable colleagues in other Western countries. Although this has changed recently, with some widely publicized exceptionally high salaries and share remunerations for newly hired top managers in large firms, generally speaking, the difference between top salaries and bottom wages is smaller in only a very few countries.

Incomes   In the Netherlands, income is normally regarded as
a highly private issue. One doesn't mention one's salary, and it is
taboo to ask anyone theirs, not only colleagues but also relatives
and friends. Indirect indicators are felt to be enough: car, living
area, holiday destination and other status symbols.

Taxes   The tax system undoubtedly helps net salaries to stay
about the same: top income is taxed 60%, almost twice the
percentage for lower salaries! Holland has a favourable tax climate
for foreign investment, but for Dutch citizens, private income of
any kind, including family wealth and inheritances, is taxed quite
heavily if larger amounts are involved.

Needless to say, quite a few people look for ways to evade
taxes. Many of those with good salaries move to Belgium and
further away, but these and other foreign tax constructions are
frowned upon by the general public and therefore not talked
about.

Smaller-scale tax evading (e.g. by hiring illegal workers to do
jobs in the house) is widely done, and it is estimated that the
'black market' economy runs into billions of guilders. Yet one
cannot say that tax evasion is a mass movement. A very practical
reason may be that the well-organised Dutch bureaucracy makes
this difficult to do, but probably equally important is the fact that
the tax system works in accordance with the Dutch egalitarianism
value.

Everyone can see what is done with the taxes, for one's own
comfort and that of others. Many public facilities are subsidised:
public transport, education, theatre groups, museums, libraries,
facilities for the disabled, housing schemes and rents for low-
income earners. It costs the state billions of guilders each year,
but it is generally accepted as a good reason for the tax system.
Other major tax expenditures go to various, and for international
standards quite sumptuous, social benefits for all sorts of people
who have the bad fortune of being unemployed, in poor health,
old, etc. In Dutch culture, such conditions are usually considered
not to be the people's own fault, and therefore they should be
given the chance to 'act normal' also.

It also saves the taxpayers a lot of trouble: poverty, people not
insured against sickness, social upheaval in general. With the

exception of a certain degree of poverty, such phenomena are unknown in Holland.

Foreigners quite often react in surprise to all this, like this Czechoslovakian did just before the communist system in his country collapsed: *'The Netherlands is more socialist than the 'socialist' countries. The way they take care of the weak here! Take ill people for example: one may be ill for some weeks a couple of times a year, they just keep paying you. The unemployed get benefits and something extra for their holidays. It is very social here, in some respects too much, which causes people to abuse it easily.'*

Of course, no one likes receiving the blue tax envelopes, but all in all the Dutch public feels the system to be right. The majority of the Dutch silently agree that justice and social harmony are well worth paying for. Then we can all act normal.

Origins of egalitarianism　It is time now to look at the origins of this core value of Dutch culture. The sense of being morally equal originates from, and at the same time perpetuates, the rather flat pyramid of Dutch society. In his book *Culture's Consequences,* prof. Hofstede indicates 'power distance' in the Netherlands to be among the lowest in the world, only surpassed in the Scandinavian countries.

Hofstede's explanation refers mostly to the protestant character of Dutch society, but many foreign observers see the natural Dutch environment as the origin of this low hierarchy. Some stress the fact that in a low lying, reclaimed country like Holland, everyone is equally threatened by water, but others object: what about Bangladesh, the Nile Delta, parts of China, which are not so equality-minded!

Highly controversial though it is to directly link a nation's mentality to its scenery or climate, the explanation might be found indirectly in a related aspect: the social structures that the Dutch developed to fight the everlasting threat of water.

The watercontrol boards *(waterschappen)* that cover the whole country, were founded already in the 13th century and are therefore older than virtually all other public institutions, and were very flat in structure also. These self-help organisations consisted of a group of farmers or fishermen who chose a leader from their own ranks. This *'dijkgraaf'* (literally: the count of the dyke) was in fact a 'primus inter pares' who could only exercise power when it was needed during high tides or threatening storms. For centuries, all (male) inhabitants of the *waterschap* had to contribute to the construction, guarding and repair of the dykes. Since all had a vital interest in doing so, they contributed manpower and finance. Thus, people made themselves so to speak 'physically autonomous' in a hierarchically very low structure.

On a more philosophical level, there are other contributing factors. As early as the late 1300s, a religious movement ('The Brethren of Common Life') in the (then Catholic) Low Countries called for a humble, spiritually oriented life rather than the luxury that developed among the clergy. A hundred years later, Erasmus' Humanism pleaded for humane, just and non-violent behaviour towards all living souls, even including animals. Ideas like these influenced Dutch Protestantism and later permeated society through wider and wider circles of general education.

In the mid-1500s Calvinism (a particularly strict version of Protestant Christian faith) was very successful in becoming the dominant religion. It emphasised that all people are born imperfect, prone to sin, and that one should work lifelong on improving oneself in order to persuade God to forgive this original sin. This applies to everyone, meaning that on a moral level we are all equally bad, brothers in sin, disregarding one's social position. In the Bible Jesus indicates that a wealthy or powerful person can be a greater sinner at heart than a repentant thief or a prostitute. Everyone, therefore, should scrutinise his own behaviour for the flaws of sin, and work on them. It was a call for individual soul-searching rather than for collective expressions of faith. To this day, Calvinistic churches are rather empty, undecorated and white on the inside, stimulating an individualistic, introspective mood.

The dividing line between Protestantism and Catholicism in the Netherlands roughly coincides with the one between the lower and higher parts of the country. Could it be that the fast spread of the Calvinistic socioreligious equality and autonomy was somehow related to the physical autonomy that the lowlanders had accomplished with their waterworks?

Be that as it may, Calvinism became a leading force in the political struggle that gained the Dutch independence from Habsburg Spain. In all but name Calvinism reached the status of a state religion, while Catholicism had to go into hiding. Calvinism kept its dominant position[2] up to about 1850, when a church rift divided the Protestants into two separate denominations, later followed by others. At the same time, Catholics were allowed to surface again, soon followed by the emerging socialist movements.

Religion remained a factor of great influence in Dutch society up to about 1960. Then social changes, drastically reacting to existing power structures, rather suddenly eroded religion, turning the Netherlands into one of the least church-going nations of Europe today. Calvinism currently is practised by only some 8% of the population, most of them rural[3], yet its concept of moral equality still permeates many aspects of Dutch society.

1. For detailed factual and legal information on this and other labour regulations, please refer to 'Employers and Labour Relations in the Netherlands', a 1995 publication by the Dutch General Employers' Association AWV, P.O.Box 568, 2003 RN Haarlem, the Netherlands.

2. Not in the southern provinces of Brabant and Limburg, see chapter 9.

3. See chapter 9.

Chapter 3

ON DIRECTNESS AND CRITICISM

'Straight through the sea'
(Dutch saying, praising directness)

No flattering please   Just as all people are considered more or less equal, so are their ideas. In Dutch society, everybody has the right to say what they think, no matter what their social position, and thus opinions are easily voiced. They are also listened to, albeit their thoughts are certainly not always accepted! But no one need fear to speak up, as sanctions are not likely to follow (except being frankly criticised). Superiors cannot really put someone down for merely stating his or her opinion, and although it happens of course, people are not supposed to use other people as stepping stones. That would be considered unfair: one's *own* performance should be the only criterion.

Being straightforward is one thing, but the way to express such thoughts is another matter. In some languages people prefer voicing disapproval with terms like 'not so good' or euphemisms like 'interesting'. In the case of the Dutch, criticisms are not concealed, not wrapped up in many words. Their direct ways of expressing themselves can be shocking to foreigners. An observer from Britain: *'British people will not say what they think, except to very good friends. Here in Holland it may happen that someone asks you: why is your hair so long, why do you wear that tie with that shirt? I wouldn't be surprised if they told me: what an awful tie you're wearing!*

We British always worry whether we do the right thing, whether we behave well. The Dutch don't.'

No, they don't; in fact, they rather appreciate honest criticism over flattery and compliments. A better understanding of this explicit criticism requires some explanation of the structure of society and the Dutch way of making decisions. Very few groups of people in the Netherlands, rallied round whatever issue, can create a majority, and even if they do, there will always be factions or individuals with a mind of their own. A BBC film described Dutch society as one of 'little boxes in a land of little squares'.

No 'little box' has absolute power, so any decision, whether in companies, in Parliament, in the town hall or in a local volleyball club, involves debate and then: compromise, water in the wine. If people don't clearly bring forward their ideas, preferably backed up with sound argumentation, none of those ideas will appear in the final decision. So opinions are expressed, loudly and clearly, especially if they do not concern private emotional matters. And one had better not give in until the final decision arrives.

Critical attitudes and strong opinions are clearly expressed.

Large groups of the Dutch population find a short and unequivocal word quite enough: e.g. the words *'waardeloos'* (worthless, lousy) and *'fout'* (wrong) are often used, also among colleagues.

Rude words   Considerable numbers of people, most of all youngsters, use rude words (spelled with three letters in Dutch) to express dislike and, sometimes shocking to English speakers, also English four-letter words, which being foreign, don't sound quite so crude in Dutch ears. Even when no rude words are used, Dutch opinions may come across very strong. Yet the Dutch speaker only wishes to be fair to you. Part of this misunderstanding may also stem from translation: the Dutch language has several short words that 'soften' opinions ('maar', 'even', 'een beetje') but once translated they don't mean much, so Dutch people whose English is not perfect just leave them out. The literal English translation then comes across far more bluntly than the Dutchman ever wanted it to sound.

Striving for perfection   In business, bad words are not used, but critical attitudes do prevail. Your Dutch counterparts will inspect any proposal or performance in detail, ask questions, give their opinion only slightly concealed. This leads foreigners who are not used to such directness to call the Dutch 'opinionated' and 'arrogant'. But please remember: you are free and even expected to do exactly the same. It is up to you to develop similar frankness! 'Straight onto the man', the Dutch might then describe you, and you should take it as a compliment.

Dutch English   Native speakers of English should realise that Dutch people's English is seldom 100% perfect. Linguistic misunderstandings may easily increase a native English speaker's impression that the Dutch are blunt or arrogant. A good example is the difference in meaning between 'to propose' and 'to suggest'. A Dutch manager found his English colleagues irritated when innocently he used 'proposal' (a rather compelling hint) when he had actually meant 'suggestion' (a creative idea as good as any other one).

So the Dutch speak up. Especially in comparison with Asian cultures, loss of face is of little concern to many of them. You ask their opinion and you get it, clearly stated, no obscuring or disguising for politeness' sake. The Dutch have learned to deal with this, but many foreigners are shocked by the straightforwardness. They often perceive it as 'blunt', hostile, unfriendly.

But here we come to a paradox: the Dutch will only tell you all this if they take you seriously, if they feel you to be close enough, in the same 'little box' as they are. So, strange as it may sound, directness and criticism mean: appreciation, belonging, you are one of us, we accept you as more or less equal, a good match.

If they don't feel this, they will observe you but not say much. In Dutch society, basically, one should leave other 'little boxes' alone: live and let live. But we, here in our box, must strive for perfection and help each other in doing so. How can anyone improve if they overlook their imperfections? So the Dutch tell each other what's imperfect still.

In Dutch culture, imperfections are a challenge, something that must be overcome by stubborn hard work: it *must* be perfect! An observer from Iceland: *'Dutch people are nice, but they criticise other people too often and too fast. Even when they discuss a match they won, they will constantly talk about the five minutes that things went a bit less. I don't know whether this is because they all know how to do things better, or because they just want to fuss.'*

The Dutch will analyse anything new. The good aspects are soon taken for granted: perfect?, OK, put it aside, not interesting anymore. They go on looking for *im*perfections. These will be pointed out immediately and discussed: *'When you go to a concert or a theatre here, immediately afterwards everything is analysed, verbally cut to pieces.'* (Ireland)

Now don't think that criticism is always given in such serious ways; it can be wrapped up in jokes, irony, sarcasm. Self-mockery and self-irony are also greatly appreciated. Picturing yourself small, making your performance relative is in line with the equality issue. It helps to make greatness more palatable to the Dutch. The Dutch verb *'relativeren'* is often used: making things relative, seeing them in their right perspective. This becomes particularly evident when a Dutch person receives a compliment. In line with the widespread critical attitudes, compliments are *not* easily extended, since perfection is distrusted. If they are, the receiver will usually wave them aside, or 'make them relative' with self-mockery, probably uneasy about too much perfection. In most cases 'good' will do. Superlatives like 'terrific', 'great' and the like should be reserved for very special occasions only. A business woman from Hungary dryly observed: *'Good news is not welcomed here.'* Perfection is merely duty, working on imperfections forms one's real task in life. So: tell us what's still wrong, please. The Icelander went on: *'They need to have a problem. If they don't have one, they'll look for it, because with a problem you can discuss: "How are we going to solve it?"'*

Task-oriented and serious The Dutch are task-oriented. What matters is that the product, the service, the performance is improved. In this striving for perfection, the product or, if need be, the whole organisation is verbally dismantled into its smallest components. Anything faulty is discussed, taken out and replaced by a better version, and then it's all reassembled. New, closer to perfection. Companies, ministries, organisations are restructured all the time, roads are under constant repair, houses are redone, office furniture is changed, computer systems updated. (Such changes are often accompanied by training programmes for managers and employees. The Dutch management training sector is well-developed and thriving!)

And then when things are improved, let's not spend too much time on congratulating ourselves but get back to work, there is more to do. This may sound rather gloomy. However, although the Dutch are serious, most of them are not depressed by this. Colleagues who just had critical discussions about their common performance may go and have a pint together afterwards (but just one, see chapter 8). The discussion may go on at the bar, and no one gets offended. Although the Dutch may not show it, they quite enjoy all this working on improvement. They talk about it, long and thoroughly, possibly intensely, but rarely with dramatic gestures or very loud voices. Such drama would undermine the speaker's point of view, rather than strengthen it. Not too many emotions, please. And no superlatives. *'Sometimes the Dutch get on my nerves, their mentality is so different from mine. They are very reliable but terribly serious. So down to earth and cold. They observe life with their brains, everything goes according to the rules. I miss the Czech openness and spontaneity, the gaiety. Dancing and singing don't come easy to the Dutch.'* (Czech Republic)

Indeed, it doesn't, certainly not in working hours. Most of the year the Dutch come across as very serious, looking earnest, rarely joking, smiling only occasionally. Working hard and concentrated, with a well-developed sense of duty and responsibility (and computers and machines helping them), they have the highest productivity per worked hour in the world. Lucky for them they have long (and paid) holidays. *'The Dutch are serious and they take everything seriously. You must be careful with jokes, they may easily get it wrong. This serious attitude is good for business, Dutch people are good at that.'* (Nigeria)

In spite of all this seriousness, the Dutch are apparently quite happy: they scored very high in an Europe-wide survey on contentment with life. Someone from Tanzania comments: *'I like the way they smile here'.*

When you do see Dutch people being very enthusiastic ('going out of their roof' is the Dutch expression for this), it is usually in private, in the company of friends or relatives. In public, it takes a valid reason, ranging from football matches through Queen's Day to bachelors' parties, and most often a drink or two (or ten). The result is not always pleasant to witness. Like me, you'll probably prefer to avoid football stadiums on the night of the match!

Back at work, what counts is that the product will be improved, the target reached. The constant striving for perfection is a (sub-conscious) part of Dutch upbringing. People deal with criticism and a lack of compliments in a somewhat detached manner: this is me and that over there is what I do, so feel free to shoot.

Conflicts and decisionmaking   Sometimes, of course, people do get hurt or angry. If 'talking it over' doesn't help anymore, there are various other calm solutions: ignore each other or, if a meeting is unavoidable, organise to keep these people out of each other's way. This may involve lengthy meetings, but rarely any violence. On a more collective scale, the same also applies.

'In other countries conflicts easily escalate. Here people stay calm. The company council, the trade unions and the company directors take decisions in relative harmony.' (Switzerland)

Labour conflict, strikes and such are not unknown in the Netherlands, but less time is lost with them than in most other European countries. Collective labour agreements often include no-strike agreements. If not, strikes may only take place after serious negotiating has failed, by court permission. The trade unions will support them in that case. 'Wild' strikes, unlawful and not backed up by the unions, happen occasionally, but without payment, and they never last long. New negotiations are bound to follow. Given this fact, merely threatening with strikes can be enough to re-start stagnant negotiations.

Conclusion: solving conflicts or problems in Holland just takes a lot of talking, so please have your opinion ready, and state it, clearly!

Long discussions have always been part of Dutch culture. In the old days they dealt with the sermon, after church. Nowadays they are concerned with politics, street crime, new legislation, anything, anywhere: over lunch, at parties, in sidewalk cafés, on the camping ground. And on television, of course. Compared with American ones, Dutch talk shows are – again – quite serious, lacking much glamour. During such a debate, on TV or elsewhere, one may see quite earnest faces, both among the speakers and the public, but at the same time debate is rather fun to the Dutch, very serious fun. It is like a game of chess, thoughtful and precise, everybody calmly waiting for their turn and yet exciting. Reflecting Holland's social pluriformity, widely differing points of view may and will be expressed, so it can take quite some time before any conclusion is reached. You will not be surprised to hear that Holland has many political parties and that their debates take up much time, sometimes lasting into the wee hours.

Lengthy decisionmaking may be threatening companies, too, involving people of different levels. Although in recent years a more speedy decisionmaking process has come to be appreciated and stimulated, to many a foreigner's taste it still takes far too long, as for this American observer: *'In the [Dutch] company where I work, I exclaimed: for heaven's sake, let's stop talking about it and DO something!'*

There is also a good side, however, as expressed by this Frenchman: *'Yes, decisionmaking in Holland lasts awfully long, but everybody is heard in the process and once the decision is finally taken, all seem to recognise their point of view in it somehow, so they will implement it.'*

And that is exactly what counts: everyone consulted and involved. This happens at all levels, including the way the government deals with private enterprise. The same Swiss person quoted above observed: *'The agreements that (Dutch) enterprise made with the government are unique. In every other country, environmental laws are dictated by the authorities, which then evokes resistance from the companies involved.'*

A land of compromise and moralism   Holland is a land of talking it out and compromise, in other words. Compromise is essential in maintaining social peace and getting people to work for the common cause. Compromise at all costs: if extra expenses are needed to satisfy all parties (provided their arguments are sound), so be it.

A barrier of compromise   In the 1970s and 1980s a giant dam in the southwestern province of Zeeland was constructed (the Oosterscheldedam). People wanting it closed for safety were opposed by people who came up with economic and ecological arguments for keeping it open. After a long debate, all parties won, at a much larger cost than foreseen. The compromise was: an open construction but closeable within half an hour. Another example, from 1996: the high-speed train from Paris to Amsterdam will go through an eight km long and 900 million guilders tunnel beneath the ecologically worthwhile meadows of the Dutch polder landscape. On the other hand the high speed train will not pass by The Hague, the seat of Parliament, for economic reasons (too expensive).

Social harmony and compromise between conflicting opinions bought for dear money in a nation of reputedly money-minded people.

After centuries of deep religiousness, quite some moralism has crept into the criticisms of the Dutch. Wagging the index finger is a recurring phenomenon: you are wrong, I am right. Although unpopular, moralising happens often, in the country itself and, coming as a shock sometimes, also in international dealings. There are regular calls for boycotting this or that country for its poor environmental policy, disrespect of human rights, or other abuses the Dutch public disapproves of. Governments abroad have received thousands of postcards from Dutch people protesting (in organised campaigns) against racist incidents or nuclear testing or whale fishing.

On a more official level, Dutch government functionaries have had the honour of being told by foreign hosts (behind the scenes, usually) that some of their opinions had better be kept to themselves. Some painful incidents occurred. Companies, too, can be scolded for misdemeanours like polluting, investing in undemocratic countries, for using the wrong materials. Demonstrations, boycotts and in a few cases even some violent protest follow. Companies where accidents happened during production nowadays immediately publicise this with extensive apologies, rather than wait for the public storm to burst. Of course, they promise to improve their production methods. Such action is appreciated, and most protest dies away.

Some foreigners appreciate the critical stance of the Dutch, like this Nigerian: *'I appreciate the critical attitude of Dutch society. I like the way the media tackle touchy subjects, how they sometimes attack one another and how the authorities are open to the public. That is a good element in democracy.'*

Surely there are still imperfections. Foreign expatriates complain about government bureaucracy, slow service, short banking and shopping hours (these were relaxed only very recently), unclear procedures when plumbers and electricians come to their homes, poor facilities for working women (see chapter 8). The Dutch may complain about all this and much more, plus the weather of course. But then, see it as a national sport.

Historical backgrounds   We now turn to the historical background of Dutch outspokenness. For over 200 years, until the French installed a puppet kingdom, the country was a federal republic. It had emerged out of the 16th century revolt against Spanish rule, so it was a kind of 'self-made' country. People felt their leaders to be appointed by themselves rather than absolute monarchs, as in the neighbouring countries. Since Calvinism coincided with great prosperity, the Dutch felt they were under special divine protection, and foreign admiration of the republic's modern institutions contributed to a sense of moral superiority.

The republic was pluriform from the start; no one group could impose its will. Whether interpretations of the Bible, colonial policy or new laws and taxes, everything was discussed, and differing views had to be accommodated somehow: compromise.

A few more authoritarian periods ended with riots and upheaval. Authority was all right as long as the public felt it to be ordained by God, then they obeyed.

The most recent large-scale questioning of authority occurred in 1966, when the general dissatisfaction of the younger generation brought down university deans and mayors. Freedom-addicted Amsterdam led the way. With one or two exceptions, these social changes happened rather peacefully but with very long discussions indeed. There was a new element, however: it all involved a good deal of mockery and laughter, which was the ideology of the youth movement: playfulness, fantasy, down with all those serious and solemn autocrats.

More humour has come into Dutch public culture since the 1960s. Irony, satire and self-mockery became part of many political campaigns and social movements, even of advertising, and are appreciated by the public. *'You should not disturb a brooding hen'*, a female and rather stout minister of social affairs told her functionaries on strike, indicating she already had solutions in mind. All of the strikers laughed, the TV public loved it, and the problem was soon solved.

An organisation called *Loesje* (a random girl's name) uses satirical posters to mock fixed or outdated opinions still taken for granted. They make people laugh at themselves and at government bureaucracy. The press awarded them a prize for opening fresh ways of communication and it was handed out by... a government minister.

All in all, the effectiveness of criticism and outspokenness is considered far more important than the status of either the speaker or the person commented upon. Some basic standards of common decency should be respected, of course, but Dutch standards in this field may surprise foreigners!

Chapter 4

PRAGMATIC AND MONEY MINDED

'Fried air'
(Dutch slang expression for pompous talk
or useless objects)

The Dutch are practical people, with a highly developed sense of realism in combination with 'down to earth-ness'. Dutch art reflects this: in the 1600s artists like Rembrandt and Vermeer painted common folks during their simple everyday activities, in the 1800s Van Gogh painted poor peasants. Mondriaan is famous for his colourful grid-patterns, which can be interpreted as abstractions of Dutch man-made, rational landscapes with flower bulbs and canals.

A Russian translator of Dutch literature observed: *'Dutchmen have to consider every step they take, otherwise they run into a wall, a fence, a corner. They are forced to be concrete, and they actually like the concreteness produced by their lack of space. But at the same time they want to break out. Look at all those canals in Holland, they fade away into endlessness.'*

Indeed, the Dutch like concreteness. Task-oriented, they tend to focus on contents and purpose rather than on aspects like personal contact, prestigious appearance, ceremony and circumstance. Act normal and be useful. Practical aspects like time schedules, price, and other concrete conditions are dealt with in great detail, in word and in action.

Business comes before pleasure Dutchmen tend to start a business contact without allowing much time for getting to know the counterpart. Often, a simple 'good morning, how are you today' is felt to be enough. When people don't bother to do even this, even the Dutch may find this too fast. 'Invading the house with the door' is the expression used for such impatient behaviour. Yet an unceremonious 'let's get down to business'-attitude is the usual procedure. Within minutes Dutchmen start focusing on the purpose of the get-together, the qualities of the product involved, the details of the transaction. To business partners from more relation-oriented cultures, this seems rather impatient and unsophisticated, on top of the bad feelings about directness: *'The Dutch have a trading mentality: they want to see results immediately.'* (Pakistan)

Luckily, the Dutch can usually make up for these objections by being trustworthy and punctual in the follow-up.

Especially in the business world, Dutch people do not appreciate vagueness, castles in the air, philosophical talk that fails to lead back to earth. Ideas and activities are all right as long as they lead to practical and measurable effects.

In more relation-oriented cultures, business people may like to position themselves by hinting at their good education, their prestigious family backgrounds, their power as a boss, their good relations with politicians. All this does not appeal to the Dutch, rather it makes them feel uneasy. They tend to find such circular movements irrelevant and a waste of time, possibly even pompous or cocky. It is the *product* they are interested in, the transaction, the successful business cooperation. If your product is good (and the price of course, see below), they'll be happy trading with you.

In business encounters with the Dutch it is therefore advisable to stick close to the concern of the day. Do not dwell on subjects like history, philosophy, the wonderful architecture of the capital city. Also, don't spend more than the absolute minimum amount of time on your personal background, only casually mention any prestigious contacts you have outside business. Of course, most Dutchmen would politely go along for a bit, but probably wonder why you are bringing this up: you were here for business, weren't you?

So, within minutes: show your product, talk of its qualities, stress its usefulness for the customer, bring out the prospectuses, ask their specific needs, show them how you can meet these, answer their questions and mention the price. Your Dutch counterpart will not say it, but will think: 'That's the right guy, clear and direct, coming to the point!'

And of course, don't be shocked by critical questions: remember that nothing can be perfect!

Now don't think the Dutch shrink away from philosophy, debate or fun. They like it, but such issues are felt to belong to times such as outside business hours, afterwards, at the golf club, at a company reception, in the break of a management training programme. 'Business comes before pleasure', the expression goes.

Do not waste money!   An important part of the pragmatic approach to business is of course: money. The Dutch proverbially use the Scottish as examples of tightness with money, stinginess, but when the Scotch protest, they plus other foreigners point at the Dutch. The English language has the expression 'going Dutch' while Belgians tell quite a few jokes about money-tight Dutchmen. The following quotations are from German and Norwegian observers, for a change: *'It is striking how there's always a price tag attached here. In Holland people immediately ask what things cost. Whether it is the shortage of prison cells, a new railway line or a UN building in The Hague: how much will it cost? That is a kind of scrooginess you also meet on a small scale.'*

'Sometimes I find the Dutch very, very mean. I sometimes feel they're only thinking of money and how to save it.'

It is true the Dutch are money minded. Seven centuries of trading must have penetrated the national psyche. Selling and buying, negotiating, getting a better price represent fun to the Dutch, very serious fun. Some nations may challenge fortune by gambling, the Dutch do it by chasing bargains, be it small scale in private or large scale in the world. It's a sport, one expects the opponent to be equally cunning, and one is proud after winning. Again, the task is the purpose, any hurt feelings are side-effects only.

There is an old complaint about the Dutch by an English observer who apparently struck very bad luck both at work and in private life:

'In love and in trade, the fault of the Dutch
is giving too little and asking too much.'

Leaving the love aspect for more private investigation, we will concentrate on the trade issue. Although the Dutch may not exactly like that rhyme, they'll probably think: too bad for him, he should have bargained better!

One doesn't speak of a good selling price of course – like salaries, one's profits are a well-kept secret – but a good buying price is often stated as an extra asset to the purchase, in business as well as privately. Any great expense is carefully considered beforehand, in government, in business, in the family. So in the unlikely case that your price is accepted easily, you must be selling too cheap!

Following the biblical advice on 'using one's talents', Calvinism taught that profits should not lead to frivolous enjoyment. Loans and credits for such purposes were also frowned upon, one should only spend what is already earned by virtuous hard work. Cash was the message, and to quite some degree it still is: getting cash from bank dispensers in the streets is more popular than using cheques and credit cards, to the distaste of expatriates. Dutch chain stores are experimenting with digital 'debit cards' that can be used for small transactions.

It is possible that this cash orientation is also a consequence of trading worldwide in times before and places outside any banking network, which demanded immediate payment in cash.

Yet there are paradoxes, even when it comes to money. This nation that eagerly accumulates money and saves it, also spends one of the world's highest percentages of GNP on international schemes like development cooperation, relief funds, UN peace missions, the support of ecological projects worldwide. Privately, the Dutch raise large sums of money in televised actions for all kinds of charity. Money collectors for local or international charity campaigns rarely ring the doorbell in vain.

So expenditure for pleasure doesn't come easy to Dutchmen, but people who are perceived as underprivileged 'victims of circumstances' can most often count on help from the Dutch public. Even animals, landscapes and lifeless things can be in a position that calls for assistance. The Dutch support many different projects. A few random examples: sports' facilities for the disabled, campaigns against child labour in far away countries, the survival of vulnerable nature areas in Holland or at the South Pole, the repair of dilapidated museums, etc. Such support is given both through private donations and by government financing, and it deeply satisfies the Dutch: how useful!

Of course, there are critical people pointing out that at least part of the money is meant to create business or job opportunities in Holland itself, or that the surviving forest may be the next holiday destination for travel-loving Dutchmen. But such opinions are far less widely publicised...

A lady from Mauritius, having lived in Holland for some 20 years, told me: *'I have come to the conclusion that the Dutch are not stingy after all. They just hate to waste anything.'*

Wasting, that is the keyword. If the Dutch find expenses necessary, useful, well worthwhile, then they spend. If they feel them to be a luxury, extravagant, superfluous, then they're tight. This is reflected in advertising, for all but the top layer of the market. Most often the price argument is more strongly stressed than aspects like quality, status, usefulness.

In Calvinism, traditionally, one did not spend for enjoyment, one saved or re-invested. Even nowadays, when money (or energy, time) is spent on useless things, the Dutch will comment: *'Zonde!'*. This religious term, meaning 'sin', says enough about the background of this attitude. Usefulness and saving made up Calvinism's message. Small wonder that for centuries Amsterdam was Europe's banking centre. Amsterdam still is a respectable financial centre, and the Dutch still save.

Of course, with the general prosperity and relaxation in moral attitudes since the 1960s, spending has become easier for the Dutch, also morally, and you will see the nation happily shopping and consuming. Even so, the Dutch are still great money savers. The extensive and internationally successful Dutch banking and finance sector is based on very large amounts of money safely tucked away in bank accounts, shares, property. In recent years so much money has been put into private arrangements for old age/pension plans that producers of consumer goods worry about decreasing expenditure, some complain of a 'buyers' strike'.

In many other ways the Dutch 'keep an apple for thirst', as they say. The government workers' pension fund (ABP), now privatised, has one of the world's largest investment capitals (in 1995: 195 billion guilders), disproportionate to the country's ranking in the world economy. Almost every Dutch household is well insured against any mishap, so Dutch insurance companies too are large and operate internationally. Some things are large in Holland!

The Netherlands is a rich country, so what is the need of all this money mindedness, one might wonder. The expression 'going Dutch' and the rhyme quoted above (both British in origin) are some 300 years old. Apparently this is something very established in the Dutch character.

Of course, the practical attitudes are in line with the sense of equality and the general directness in conversation. With the present prosperity and the decline in religiousness, things are changing, but still there are many rather ascetic aspects to Dutch culture, in spite of all the cafés, amusement parks, sporting and feasting.

Food Dutch food, for instance. Food is a topic few Dutchmen even care discussing, but – as I have experienced time and again – it can be quite an issue for foreigners in the Netherlands, and not just the French: *'You Dutchmen don't find food interesting, for us Italians it is much more important. Put five or six Italians together – serious business people, good friends, whatever – and in no time they will discuss food. Not the Dutch, they have other ways of enjoying themselves.'* (Italy)

In line with the no-nonsense mentality, Dutch meals are usually simple and short: food as a kind of necessary fuel to keep one fit for performance. Long meals are a waste of time, and one doesn't talk of food during business. Small surprise that Dutch business people have the shortest lunches in Europe! If no guests are around, lunch at work will most likely be taken in the company restaurant, a sober meal of bread, thinly sliced meat and cheese, and milk. Soup, a salad or some fruit may be added, although these are already felt to be a bit of luxury. One may observe people of all levels (albeit usually not at the same table) having a fast and simple lunch, possibly buying soup or a hot snack to add to sandwiches brought from home. It's not just schoolkids, but also people in business, banking or government who may be seen with a homemade luncheon package. This is fully in line with the Dutch character: practical, cheap and ignoring hierarchy or status.

Now don't think the Dutch are unable to enjoy good food, or even that they do not taste it. You will find restaurants everywhere, full with people at the right time of day. Also at home many Dutch people take pleasure in good cooking and extensive dinners. Yet it is still uncommon for most Dutchmen to have dinner in town or to prepare a four-course meal at home on a weekday, especially not outside the Randstad.

Eating a dish more fancy than the traditional meal of potatoes, one type of vegetable plus a small portion of meat is a post-1960 development for most Dutchmen, and only due to the general prosperity is eating out no longer exceptional. When they do, the Dutch prefer more exotic cuisines than their own. Even when dinner guests are entertained at home, chances are the family has chosen a foreign recipe rather than Dutch cuisine.

Dress, glamour and elegance   Generally speaking, the approach to dress is equally pragmatic. There is a certain informality in Dutch clothing and self-presentation, mostly at lower levels but also in the business world. It is another example of sobriety appreciated by many Dutchmen but not always by foreigners. The same can be said about the low-profile character of many ceremonies in Holland.

Again, times are changing, and one might encounter more outspoken luxury nowadays, but still you will mostly find low-profile attitudes. They are considered more tasteful than glitter and gold, pomp and circumstance. Possibly this opinion by an American resident throws some light on this attitude: *'I like the smallness of things in Holland. Everything is small here, even the skyscrapers.'*

The Dutch are aware of other nations' glamour and elegance, and suffer from mixed feelings. On the one hand, their low-profile pragmatism makes them disapprove or sometimes even mock others' lavish architecture and extravagant fashion, their street strolling and emotionality. But it doesn't take a psychologist to see that at the same time they envy such *joie de vivre*. Many Dutchmen eagerly travel to such fun places, happily joining in with local lifestyles and celebrations. Within the country itself, people from the southern provinces have mixed feelings about 'Hollanders' participating in their carnival celebrations (see chapter 9). Even in northern Holland some recent hot summers brought out this other side of the Dutch.

But when one is back home in the autumn, the idea of continuing such a lifestyle turns out to be an illusion. Recently, a Dutch scientist proposed the following thesis: *'European unification might take a long time as long as Italian raincoats are elegant and Dutch ones waterproof.'* A Dutch lady who returned home after years of living abroad adds: *'It's hard staying elegant in a rainstorm with gale force seven!'*

Going Dutch   One last thing about money: 'Going Dutch'. (For those not familiar with these English expressions, both 'going Dutch' and 'a Dutch treat' mean: splitting the bill in a restaurant, each party paying its own share.) They originate from long-forgotten Anglo-Dutch hostility in the 1600s, but this quotation from the same German observer mentioned above is recent: *'You go for dinner somewhere and afterwards all expenses must be calculated: "He drank one beer more..." Terrible!'*

What about it, is it really that bad? The Dutch don't agree. They 'go Dutch' when they feel all things are equal: no difference in position or income plays a role, no special event is being celebrated, no courtesies whatsoever are necessary. Such a non-occasion is apparently what the observer witnessed (and by the way: persons fussing over one extra beer – they do exist! – are also disliked by the Dutch!)

Going Dutch occurs when colleagues eat out together for reason of both working overtime. Also, two students short on cash will apply Dutch treat, and indeed calculate that he had this dessert but she did not. A group of friends who suddenly decide to have drinks but not at anyone's particular invitation may go Dutch, as might people who see each other so often that any need for formality is gone.

In all other situations, one party will try to please the other by paying, just like anywhere else: lovers, people with guests, business people inviting you out, parents with children, a boss and her secretary. And sometimes the 'poorer' party may offer to pay, for a change, just like anywhere else.

Chapter 5

PROCEDURES AND PERMISSIVENESS

'Verboden toegang, art. 461 WvS'
(Frequently seen sign in Holland, indicating: no entrance)

Control freaks   To most foreigners, Holland comes across as an orderly country. Quite some observers attribute this to the physical features of the country. Indeed, the scenery looks organised, with straight ditches and canals, square fields and neatly arranged suburbs. Society, too, gives an organised impression, with trains (usually) running on time, the garbage collection due every Tuesday (or another day), water, light and electricity never failing, etc. It all depends on personal taste, and probably also on experience in one's home country whether one likes this or not: *'There is a certain order in Holland that makes things easier. Society functions well and is also quite stable. If the government changes, nothing else really changes. This order leaves you free to develop yourself the way you want to.'* (Chile)

When dealing with Dutchmen, in business and after hours, you will soon find that most of them are precise people. They handle things with great attention and an open eye for details, applying regulations and procedures consciously (on paper) or unconsciously (with time, daily activities, etc.). Some foreigners call the Dutch 'control freaks', others like it: *'Everything here goes in time. Two o'clock is two o'clock, not earlier, not later. I like it, it is easier. You know how things will go and you can plan your day better.'* (Zambia)

Many foreigners observe that apparently there are fixed procedures for just about everything, that there seems to be little space for improvisation, for going along with life as it comes. *'I feel Holland to be cramped, claustrophobic. Everything is cultivated, over-organised. You can't lose your way, even in a forest here you keep seeing signs like: 'To pancake restaurant turn right.'*   (South Africa)

'Even inside the house everything goes on schedule: dinner at six, coffee at seven. In Suriname we eat when we're hungry and we drink when we're thirsty.' (Suriname)

Quite some foreigners get irritated by functionaries, bank employees or greengrocers answering them *'dat kan niet'* (that's impossible) if they request some transaction that is slightly out of the ordinary.

Of course, a foreign country's red tape is always harder to handle than one's own country's bureaucracy, but even when taking this into account, the Dutch 'impossible' sounds rather forbidding, and sometimes it is meant to be.

Another Dutch word in this field really puts foreigners off: *verboden!* When speaking English, most Dutchmen will translate this word as 'forbidden' when they actually mean the more lenient sounding 'prohibited'. As the Dutch word is so close, the stricter English term pops up first. This linguistic error may easily irritate native speakers of English, reinforcing their impression of Dutchmen being blunt.

Also in the business world the Dutch are highly structured. Time arrangements and planning are important, verbal and written agreements should be followed up, written rules are applied, details are not overlooked, and in negotiations the Dutch are known to come well-informed (and expecting their counterparts to be the same!).

'In my country (Cambodia) most things are verbally agreed, in talks. Here everything is put to paper and planned long beforehand. Then you start working. And if you don't meet the planning, you have failed. In other countries they think: another day tomorrow. The culture around meetings here is quite strange to me. They hold meetings over every subject, and it is discussed ten times.' (Cambodia)

'Many organisations here are rigid. They are old and structured and it is very hard to change anything in their procedures. It is very difficult to convince people to change.' (USA)

These last two observations were made just a few years ago. Without pretending that all organisations have improved on this point now, it should be said that things are changing. 'The hot breath of the market' has reached Holland, too: with increasing competition on the European and global scenes, many companies have restructured their organisation or are doing so right now; 'deregulation' takes place voluntarily and by government policy. Also, a more market-oriented and flexible younger generation is gradually reaching the business world (and government). A Moroccan manager in Holland observes: *'Youngsters don't expect anymore to be cared for from the cradle to the grave. They realise they'll have to work for their money. You should see how temp-office workers do their utmost to get a permanent job. That makes me very optimistic about Holland's future.'*

CAO's and meetings   So things are changing, but still people from more American-style economies and from more relation-oriented cultures may perceive Dutch companies and certainly the labour market as somewhat rigid.

Again, there is a story behind all this. First, and easily overlooked: the Netherlands has quite a successful economy, which doesn't stimulate anyone to change Dutch ways. But there is a more culture-related background aspect as well. In line with the equality principle, workers not only know their rights but also pursue them. In most cases both they and their employers stick to the rules that are agreed in annually reviewed negotiations between employers' organisations, trade unions and the Ministry of Social Affairs. The ensuing 'collective labour agreement' (called CAO by its Dutch abbreviation) deals with salaries, working hours, safety and hygiene conditions, environmental standards, financial procedures, the proceedings for involving the workers' council, etc. In addition, everyone receives a detailed individual job description and is trained on the job to apply their department's rules and regulations, its administrative and financial procedures.

All this deeply satisfies the Dutch desire for clarity and security, but it may hinder flexibility in an increasingly competitive market. In combination with legal obstructions preventing private enterprise from dismissing surplus employees, whose rights are heavily protected by law, the Dutch labour market was kept inflexible. For years, international economic bodies like the Organisation for Economic Co-operation and Development (OECD) criticised the Netherlands for its rigid labour market and the financial and employment implications of its extensive social benefit system.

Changes in this area aroused strong opposition from citizens who felt threatened in their security. Political parties in Holland, of which there are plenty, dreaded losing voters, so changes had to be done carefully. Only recently it became clear that the changes that have been made since the early 1980s were fruitful, that the Dutch economy of the late 1990s creates more jobs and a higher growth than the economies of Germany or France.

Of course, the matter involves lengthy debate, which brings us back to the subject of meetings. Dutch meetings are highly structured as well, with fixed agendas, someone given the role of chairperson and sometimes an extra 'time-watcher'. Minutes are written and distributed, the previous meeting's minutes are discussed.

In addition to themselves following fixed procedures, meetings tend to produce more procedures, in order to satisfy the various views held by the participants. Given the fact that participants come well-prepared and are expected to come out strongly with their views, it may take quite some time before compromise is reached.

'I wouldn't mind missing the Dutch meeting culture. If you phone someone, unavoidably the answer is: he's in a meeting, can you phone again? That disturbed me right from the beginning of my stay. They only meet here for the sake of meeting. The positive side is that everyone is seeking consensus with one another, although often the opinions are fixed beforehand. It becomes a charade, a ritual, sponsored by coffee producers.' (Germany)

All this, generally speaking, leads to good products, solid quality standards and employees who feel involved, but outsiders may be shocked: *'There are so many procedures, to me they are a stumbling block. There is not much give and take here.'* (Singapore)

There *is* give and take, but it all happens during meetings. The real negotiating takes place *in* meetings, not before in the hallways, although of course alliances may be sought there.

'The Dutch are perfectionists, they are too strict in their demands. I also find them rigid in their dealing with time. To them it becomes a goal rather than a means.' (A Pakistani exporter to Holland)

Time and planning   Yes, the Dutch are strict about time. Five minutes late in a personal encounter will not be mentioned, and ten is excusable, but more than that demands a telephone call and rather extensive apologies. Coming early is not liked much either, and the Dutch will just make you wait. Why all this, some might ask, what's the point?

The point is that Dutch culture is a typical example of a 'monochronic' culture, meaning: one thing at the time. If you are late, the time your counterpart allocated to you will be running out by the minute, and after an hour it is over. Other people will be waiting to see your host, on another subject. 'Monochronic' people are not very good at combining two things in one, unlike polychronic people such as Italians and other southern cultures. Two things or two different people at one time make the Dutch uneasy and irritable (also in their private life).

'The Dutch don't like to work very hard, they never work longer than required.' (Japan)

Everything is relative of course. Work ethics and a strong sense of responsibility make them work hard, but a great appreciation for leisure time plus a strong family orientation make them stick to the official working hours. After that they rush away, to the shops, to their families and to their many evening activities. This is especially true for non-managerial levels. Managers do work overtime, take their work home, carry laptops to not lose one useful minute, etc. But requiring administrative or blue-collar workers to work overtime should be kept to a minimum and at best compensated some other day, or by payment. In some organisations where payment is out of the question due to eco-nomising, workers may have as many as 100 days of compensation saved, but no time to enjoy them!

A final aspect of time is planning. 'Controlling implies looking ahead', a Dutch saying goes. The Dutch try to keep everything under control, even the future. In a stable, well-organised society this is not as difficult as in some others, but it still takes careful planning. So the Dutch do just that. They plan, allocate a realistic amount of time (and money) for every part of the procedure, and on the way they check if reality fits it or not. If not – which really bothers them usually – change the plan and reschedule. This is done all the time, everywhere, and taken very seriously.

Obviously, those 100 hours of compensation time indicate that it doesn't always work, but still: planning, calculating the risks, monitoring, evaluating and re-planning, that is the way. The Dutch don't even feel that it's a procedure, it just comes naturally to them.

Although the Dutch may love challenge and adventure (chapter 7), they don't want it at home. There they prefer safety and cosiness, full control of their own lives, security. Living in a small country, lacking vast forests or wild mountains, there are no places where man can *not* get control: *'I don't like the flat scenery here, there are no surprises. You feel like God: you can control everything and see everyone's activities.'* (Ireland)

Of course, the Dutch do have their natural environment under control, with very few exceptions (floods, climate). Keeping an area below sea level dry and arable implies quite some organising, of people, of materials, of funds. Modern water control in Holland involves a mighty ministerial organisation with regional and local departments and highly professional engineers graduating from specialised universities allocated an annual budget of billions of guilders.

Perhaps this explains how the Dutch got organised initially, and present day bureaucracy may be merely an extension of this. Be that as it may, the Dutch do believe in control, in security. Not only government and business circles apply these methods, even private people (consciously or not) do it, in their finances, their career, their housing, their household. Dutch banks supply the general public with booklets on how to invest in shares, how to provide best for old age, how to finance education for the children, etc.

To people from other cultures this may sound terribly boring and calculating (and some Dutchmen agree), but it deeply satisfies most Dutch people to have a clear path to the future. And if you don't agree, they will point out to you how successful they have become by applying their procedures. Facts prove that there is general prosperity, good health – in fact, one of the world's longest life expectancies! – and excellent health care, long, good and fairly cheap education for everyone, long (paid) holidays for most people, very high car ownership and yet good public transport, the world's lowest percentage of teenage pregnancies, etc.

But at what cost, you may ask. Well, yes, at the cost of detailed registrations, procedures for all sorts of events, permits and licences needed for most enterprises, stamps, signatures and other dreary bureaucratic hassle. And of course: very high taxation! Nevertheless, a Australian pointed out: *'There is a lot of bureaucracy, but it seems to work here.'*

Freedom secured: out of control   If given the chance, they set up private organisations in ways quite similar to those of the state: be it street committees, church organisations, charitable bodies or hobby clubs; they all have rules, a president, a finance person, someone to take the minutes, etc.

Again, we come to a paradox, even Dutch rules have their exceptions! In this well-organised country, you will see bikers ignore traffic lights while drivers may pass you on the right side with a speed far above the local limit. You will see people throw away papers under a sign telling them not to, dogs not stopped from relieving themselves right on the sidewalk, etc. Are these the same rule-abiding Dutchmen we just talked of? What is this? Is it just the general decay of good manners, the disdain for political decisions, as one finds in many Western countries, or what?

'We (Russians) also have that combination of rationalism and anarchism, so typical for the Dutch. But with the Dutch rationalism dominates and anarchism is deep down, while in Russia anarchism and irrationality are at the surface.' (Russia)

Bureaucracy, rules and regulations are not the goal of life for the Dutch but practical means to achieve and maintain the security to live the way they want. So, once they feel this freedom is secured, the rules can be set aside. If this doesn't happen officially, they will just ignore them and go their own way. This happens especially in situations where nobody knows you, where your peer group is not around. So: not at home, not in one's own street, not at work.

In public, the orderly Dutch can be quite anarchistic: in traffic, in public transport, in busy shopping streets, in supermarket waiting lines, in anonymous places like two streets away from home, let alone downtown. Like everywhere else, it depends on personal style, degree of inner civilisation, time and other factors as to whether people behave like this or not. Many foreigners (and with them the politer section of the Dutch population) certainly cannot appreciate it: *'Dutch people never get out of your way, they are physically close by to you. I don't like that.'* (Australia), and: *'People are pushy here, more than in Belgium or Germany. The public in shops is downright rude.'* (USA)

May I, after apologising, hint at the difference in size and population density between the observers' countries and my own, and remind the reader that 'comfortable physical distance' is a culturally determined factor as well? That being so, yes, one sees pushing, polluting and other downright impoliteness. They are expressions of highly individualistic attitudes, disregarding other people's comfort. Needless to say that – in a country that used to have a reputation for cleanliness and order – all this leads to public complaints by politicians and private people about the loss of discipline and good manners, but complaining doesn't seem to help very much.

This brings us to the next chapter, on tolerance and indifference, but first let's conclude by looking at some final remarks on Holland's small size and cramped space: *'You cannot move a centimeter here or you run into someone. And all those masses of people, so many people. I sometimes feel like a fish swimming against the current, against all those swarms of people, while I want to watch everything at ease.'* (Iceland)

'Driving is difficult here, with narrow streets and canals, and bicycles all over you.' (Canada)

'Everything is small here: the shops, the refrigerators, the houses, the toilets, the showers.' (Iran)

Chapter 6

TOLERANT OR INDIFFERENT?

'Freedom, happiness' (Dutch saying)

Many business people take at least some time to see a bit more of the country they visit, to get a taste of the local culture. Moreover, not all business people are business *travellers*. Readers may be posted in the Netherlands for some time, and they cannot fail to notice aspects of this chapter's subject: the apparently unlimited freedom, plus the generally tolerant attitudes towards it.

'I was shocked by (...) the living together of non-married people, by the loose sexual morals.' (Pakistani businessman visiting Holland regularly.)

Authority   In Dutch society, people expect and demand to be able to judge for themselves, to make their own decisions. The absence of a strong central authority or one all-encompassing religion or world view is reflected by the fact that figures of authority are hard to find. One notices few policemen in the streets, and outside the barracks military uniforms can only be seen when soldiers travel home for the weekend. Uniforms are easily felt to be pompous or even slightly ridiculous, certainly for people without real authority, like waiters or clerks. (Remember: the contents is important in Dutch culture, not external appearance!)

'People here don't seem to feel much respect for police officers or for people in uniforms. They just talk to them or ask questions. It is all very simple and open, very normal.' (Argentine)

'Especially Amsterdam is very liberal. But not just liberal, there is a simple logic to it. For instance: riding a bike down a one-way street against the traffic. In the beginning, when I saw someone do that, I thought: how can you do that! Now I know: it is the quickest way. When I myself did it the first time – I felt very naughty – a police car saw me and the officer gestured towards me. So I started apologising, but he just said: look, we're coming from the right side, you from the wrong, so move up a bit. That was all! Just plain logical.' (United Kingdom)

Dutch authorities know that they are critically inspected by the public, and behave accordingly: low profile. If problems can be solved through calm discussion, they will usually do so, knowing that afterwards the same groups will still be around. Only in extreme cases will they make use of their power, if really necessary with violence. But that is rare, and mostly restricted to dealing with heavy criminals, political extremists, stubborn house squatters and the like.

For the rest, people live the way they want, especially in the large cities. Within certain wide limits (set by laws based on compromise!), there is much freedom for highly individual behaviour, and little repression.

Live your own life All kinds of lifestyles are openly expressed: political views, artistic tastes, sexual preferences, protest behaviour, etc. It is all quite visible in public behaviour, fashion, hairstyles, etc. Not everyone likes it, but it is widely felt to be a basic human right. People may smile at what they see, indifferently shrug their shoulders or sourly criticise. But interference is frowned upon (although of course some violent reactions do occur, afterwards widely criticised as 'intolerant'). *'Here in Holland I have space to breathe. I can lead my own life. Nobody troubles me, I feel one among many. I love that freedom. Life here is as it should be. I like the way everybody here is independent.'* (Tanzania)

'The Dutch are very proud of their political culture, of their talent to get things done and to find negotiable solutions to their problems. They have a special feeling for practicality, based on self-confidence and trust in others, authority included. At the same time they know that authorities can make mistakes too. This gives them a kind of tolerance towards other people's failures, and space to act for themselves.' (Brazil)

But also: *'There is so much freedom and permissiveness here that sometimes it causes clashes between us and our children.'* (India)

The undisputed champion city of this social freedom is Amsterdam, where just about 'anything goes'. Foreigners react amusedly or shocked, reflecting very much what they are or aren't used to at home. Tens of thousands of foreigners have migrated to Amsterdam to join in with a kind of freedom they may not enjoy in their own country: *'In Amsterdam they like art (...). I appreciate Amsterdam a lot: it offers me knowledge and culture, it is a cultured city. It is easy for me to live and work here. Especially these last years: the city is getting more international and I find that people must think internationally.'* (Hong Kong)

'No, coming from Tokyo to Amsterdam was not like coming to a village. Amsterdam has it, Tokyo doesn't. Tokyo is nice to look at, but in an artificial, superficial way. People there are interested only in buying things, clothes especially. Amsterdam may be more gross on the outside, not as sophisticated, but there is more culture, it goes deeper.' (Japan)

Political system: pluriformity   It is hard to understand this freedom, these liberal attitudes, without looking at the political system, of which we will only give a very general outline. With two centuries of tradition as a federal republic, centralised authoritarian rule has never lasted long in the Netherlands. After regional autonomy, political and religious pluriformity took root in the Dutch political system. More than 20 political parties participate in each national election, some five or six of them playing major roles.

Pluriformity was given a new start with the rapid social change that occurred beginning in the 1960s. In just 30 years the country saw the break-up of the former small-scale society. The existing clearly defined groups with a large degree of personal contact and internal control gave way to an anonymous and mostly urban society where individuals follow very different and often opposing lifestyles. The 1960s and later decades saw the rise of well-educated generations which question authority and want to live the way they feel is right (having the means to realise it), unhampered by old conventions (but soon developing new ones).

This is not essentially unique, of course, it occurs in all Western societies, but perhaps it is a bit stronger in the Netherlands. First, because pluriformity has such historical roots here, and second, because unlike many other countries there isn't really a clear majority ideology, especially not on a national scale. Third, perhaps because the Dutch social benefit system allows non-conforming individuals a greater freedom from the demands of the labour market.

People can and do choose from (and swap between) a wide range of lifestyles, based on various combinations of class and income factors, religious or ideological views, personal preferences and subcultures. Each group has its norms and values, its approved standard behaviour and its frowned-upon deviations. For much of their lives people can stick to their group or hop from one to another if they wish.

So society is divided, but still the state sets the overall rules, which in the Dutch system are always the outcome of lengthy discussion and compromise between various groups. The effect is that they aren't really any particular group's rules, merely a more or less respected cocktail of differing ideas.

Freedom and non-interference   Thus, if people do not agree or do not see the need, they tend to ignore such general rules. They follow their own subcultural norms and values, and few people from other niches of society dare intervene these days, not so much out of fear but out of respect (at best) or indifference (at worst) towards the other group's norms.

All this freedom, all this non-interference, has its darker side, of course, and foreigners notice this, especially those from countries with stronger family and community ties: *'Not everyone is like that (stand-offish), but most people are. The way of life here is very sad to me. I can't get used to it, no matter how long I live here. All this strong individualism. Everyone to himself.'* (Cameroon)

'The Dutch have a mind-your-own-business type of life.' (Tanzania)

Yes, the Dutch do mind their own business. They seek their social contacts within the group they feel they belong to, people who share their norms and values, their tastes and preferences. This may keep them from meeting outsiders, which of course doesn't feel very inviting to foreigners. But visitors from Western countries are happily surprised sometimes: *'Generally speaking, people here are friendly. Not like Paris, where you can live somewhere for five years without knowing the neighbours. Here it happens that people suddenly ring your doorbell to ask whether you will come for a glass of wine. In other countries that happens only by previous arrangement, days beforehand.'* (Italy)

In my opinion, this Italian struck lucky, because the following observation from an Irish woman is probably more typical (especially in cities): *'Here you don't just drop in with a friend, you arrange a meeting in your agenda. But every time I do that, I wonder: will I feel like it that day?'*

Dutch society leaves you free to live the way you like, without much intervention by other people, including the authorities. On a hot summer's afternoon one may see many topless women on Dutch beaches. Any given day one may see police officers in Amsterdam or Rotterdam pass cafés from which hashish can clearly be smelled in the air. On Dutch TV one may watch a homosexual couple participate in show programmes along with other couples. There is parliamentary discussion on whether to legalise homosexual marriage or not. The majority is in favour, but there is hesitation on the implications of this move in the international arena. Childless couples can have children through artificial insemination. Amsterdam's Free University, although founded by Calvinists, offers psychological and medical treatment to people wanting a sex change.

Permissive society? Many foreigners (most definitely including visiting journalists) experience Holland as a free, tolerant or even permissive society. They are amazed, pleased or shocked by its open attitudes. Some are outright critical about all this freedom: *'It is shocking for us to see so much nudity on television and on the beaches. I find this a problem with our children.'* (Malaysian expatriate)

Quite often the misunderstanding prevails that anything goes in Holland, that Dutch law is endlessly tolerant. It isn't; there are limits. Quite a few things may happen out in the open, but this doesn't always mean they are legal. Often, they are officially illegal but tolerated in practice.

Regarding the above examples, one might say that after the 1960s most matters concerning sexuality and nudity are no longer regulated by Dutch legislation, since personal freedom is guaranteed in the constitution. Even so, certain kinds of pornography are definitely illegal (which is not the same as non-existent!), nudity may be allowed on beaches but not elsewhere, prostitution may be tolerated in some parts of the city but not in others.

Dutch law deals with more sensitive issues like abortion and euthanasia in delicate ways. The basic idea is: whether we like it or not, things like this happen anyhow, everywhere in the world. This being so, and given the fact that things happening in dark alleys tend to get out of hand, the Dutch Parliament has decided to try and legislate such matters in order to find a liveable and practically applicable framework for dealing with them, a way of combining the ideal (they don't exist) and reality (they do exist).

Lengthy debate that includes all views from the wide political spectrum of pluriform Dutch society goes on until some kind of consensus is reached. Usually, this has the character that the cake can be had and eaten at the same time. Many Dutch laws on issues like these might be translated as: 'No, this is prohibited, unless conditions 1 through 4 are fulfilled' or: 'Yes, this is allowed, but only if criteria a, b and c are met'.

Euthanasia   Let us take active euthanasia for an example, the medical ending of human life. In 1994, after years of recurring debate, Dutch Parliament took a decision on euthanasia. Rather sensationally, the foreign press announced that euthanasia. is now legal under Dutch law. It is not. Euthanasia in the Netherlands is *not* legal as such, Parliament decided, but it will not be prosecuted under the following strict conditions: (a) the patient suffers intolerably from a disease that (b) two independent doctors verify to be (c) incurable, and (d) the patient him/herself has explicitly and in full conscience expressed his/her wish to not live under such conditions. Then two independent doctors must be consulted before one of them, not against his will, ends the patient's life. Immediately afterwards, this must be reported to the authorities, not for prosecution but for registration.

This may come across as hypocritical, but any Dutchman would deny this. The Dutch perceive their legislation and less official arrangements on these subjects as finely tuned to the demands of any modern society's complexities, reflecting and encompassing widely different points of view.

Drugs policy Recently, the French government protested fiercely against Dutch drugs policy, one politician implying that Holland is a 'narco-state' threatening French and European health standards. The whole affair caused a great upheaval in Holland, infuriating many Dutch people into strong anti-French attitudes and making them more stubborn about *not* giving in to France. Some people even boycotted French wine (also in protest against the French nuclear tests in the Pacific Ocean, which the Dutch strongly oppose).

Dutch politicians and newspapers produced figures indicating the success of the nation's drugs policy in keeping the number of addicts low, in separating 'soft drugs' from 'hard drugs', etc. A Frenchman living in the Netherlands told a Dutch newspaper that drug use in France is considerable at all levels of society, but hushed up. He added: *'The Dutch reduce drugs to numbers, expenses, percentages. It is a materialistic type of consuming. The French are also materialistic but the Dutch are that in a harder way, without any wrapping. (...) Dutchmen look at things in life in their full nakedness, they see themselves with all their mistakes. The French see themselves as less sharp, they keep more of a distance, they soften things and embellish them.'*

This is a crucial cultural difference. The Dutch prefer to face reality, even when it's not nice to look at. Drug users (unlike drug dealers!) are perceived as pitiful creatures, more victim than criminal. It may not be pleasant to have them around, but they're people after all, so they must be tolerated and helped. One thing the Dutch are proud of, be it in critical ways, is their humane drug policy, their social system. They see it, basically, as a just system, maybe not flawless, but the best there is, well-considered, the outcome of a democratic process and precious compromise.

Social Benefits System   Let's take a closer look at the roots of the Dutch social benefits system. First, an observation: *'In a society (like the Dutch) where people easily get social benefits, for an unlimited period even, indifference will prevail. (...) This seems to me unfavourable, because in fact it means there is too little development in such a society. I also get irritated about the ease with which people on benefits can work 'black'. But I must admit that occasionally I do something black, too. It is so tempting, you know.'* (USA)

Obviously, the Dutch social benefits system matches Christian attitudes towards the weak in society, but it evolved through state institutions rather than through religious ones.

With the industrial revolution (in Holland that is after 1880), growing state influence and the emancipation of the working classes resulted in protective laws against 'capitalist exploitation'. First, child labour was forbidden. Soon after, restrictions were put on working hours, and basic assistance was organised for sick or wounded workers. More and more categories of people were included in protective laws. At first only government employees and private companies were involved. But as a result of the severe economic crisis in the 1930s that brought unemployment and poverty to millions, also people outside the working force were included, albeit under strict conditions.

After the enormous damage from the Second World War had been repaired, the need was felt to prevent misery for weak groups in society. A law passed in 1956 guaranteed a state pension for everyone over the age of 65. After 1960, more social benefits were set up, especially under the Labour dominated government in 1973-1977.

In those years, when the post-war generation caused a kind of 'cultural revolution' (see chapter 3), the idea prevailed that society was a human construction, that it could be perfected if people only tried hard enough. Everyone who got into trouble somehow, whether through unemployment or drugs, was considered a victim of circumstances beyond their control, deserving other people's attention and support. Welfare organisations: sprang up for all kinds of people, paid by government subsidies financed by increasingly high taxation.

In recent years the social climate has changed and hardened. There are increasing stories of abuse, society has individualised more, and the system is said to be economically damaging Holland. After 1980, various administrations have worked on reducing it, by economising, restricting the quantity and quality of benefits, bringing down taxation, privatising insurances, etc. And in recent years these measures have proven to be quite successful.

Many Dutch people see the need for this, but especially in reaction to foreign critics who cannot convince the Dutch of the superiority of their own approach, the Dutch get stubborn. Criticism is all right, but the argumentation should be sound, unemotional, not a matter of myths but based on facts. They start defending their views, and it becomes a matter of national pride. This leads us to the next chapter: the international outlook of the Dutch.

Chapter 7

THE INTERNATIONAL OUTLOOK

'He who wants to be someone, should not sit still,
but put to sea'
(Old Dutch saying)

The Dutch business world never sat still and was sailing the seas already some 700 years ago. Now, more than ever, it is wide open to contacts with the outside world and usually quite well prepared for them.

The Dutch like going places. Their small country is home to a disproportionate number of multinational companies and banks operating worldwide. There are vast Dutch investments on all continents (e.g. the Dutch are the second foreign investors in the USA). Many Dutch firms export a large share of their produce, while Dutch trucking and shipping firms are the great transporters of Europe. All in all, more than 200,000 Dutch expatriates (not counting people who have officially emigrated) work abroad, from neighbouring Germany to far away Papua New Guinea.

With its open economy, the Netherlands was among the original founders of the European Union and is still strongly advocating further integration, willing to give up certain national symbols.

Foreigners don't fail to notice this international attitude: *'I don't know any other country that is so cosmopolitan, so receptive to foreign influences like Holland. It is a friendly, open country where a foreigner feels at ease immediately.'* (Switzerland)

Think globally, act locally. More and more Dutch firms are aware of the necessity to adjust their products, their advertising and the behaviour of their representatives to the standards of the local customer market. In response to their needs, ministerial and business organisations in the Netherlands provide valuable export information, language institutes cater also for the business world, and it is not difficult to find literature and facts on even the remotest countries. For the wider public there are even TV shows featuring export opportunities in various countries.

The world: a potential market and a holiday destination
All this is not quite new, it is merely the present state of an old tradition. Already in the 1400s, the Dutch shipped merchandise
between the Baltic and Portugal. In the wake of the 16th century
Spanish and Portuguese discoveries overseas, the Dutch trade
empire expanded to Africa and the Americas, from the Arctic
Ocean to Ceylon, to Indonesia and even to isolationist Japan,
where they held a trade monopoly for centuries.

It was the Dutch who discovered Australia, who founded New
York (under its original name New Amsterdam) and Cape Town. All
over the world remains of this Dutch trade empire can be found,
in stone, in geographical names, in words left behind in local
languages and shipping terminology.

In the 17th century, the so-called 'Golden Age', many foreign
visitors came to study the achievements of the very cosmopolitan
Dutch republic. Two famous admirers were Czar Peter the Great,
in search of technology for the modernisation of his country, and
the French philosopher Descartes who studied and published in
Holland.

People prosecuted for their religion in their own country found
political refuge in the Netherlands, like the French Huguenots and
Jews from Spain and Portugal. All these visitors and immigrants
added to the international orientation of the republic.

At home the Dutch wanted snugness and careful behaviour,
overseas they found challenge and adventure. In the 19th and
early 20th centuries, colonialism was the outlet for adventurous
Dutchmen, while nowadays international business and development work offer wider horizons. Even those who live in their
home country like to break out. The Dutch greatly enjoy travelling: Dutch Saturday newspapers are filled with travel advertisements, and one encounters Dutch tourists and travellers in the
remotest countries. Back home, they are open to foreign influences, ranging from food to literature.

To the Dutch, the world has always been a potential market,
and one should know one's markets well. Dutch schools spend
more teaching hours on foreign languages than any other European nation, and foreign programs on Dutch TV, of which there
are plenty, are broadcast in the original language, with subtitling.
World geography is taught in all schools, and foreign news is
amply represented in Dutch media. Many Dutchmen are well

informed on foreign events also in non-commercial ways through personal contacts and special interest groups like Greenpeace, Amnesty International or Foster Parents Plan, which have relatively very high membership in the Netherlands.

'Many Dutchmen know much more about Africa and my country than I expected. Unfortunately it was mostly the negative aspects.' (Nigeria)

On more official levels, the Dutch government strongly advocates a role in the international field, supporting international collaboration not only in the European Union, but also in NATO and various UN peace missions.

Anti-chauvinism   With all of this, one would expect the Dutch to be awfully proud of their country. However, they are not, really. They love it dearly, but pride is not really well developed (...yet, we should say. Things seem to be changing, see below).

Generally speaking, the Dutch public is not aware of all the facts mentioned above, and people who are seem to take everything more or less for granted, assuming that the rest of the world is equally internationally minded.

'There should be more admiration for the good and beautiful things of Holland. This is such a small country and yet there are world personalities in the fields of art, literature, sports, film. Why aren't they proud of it, I am! The Dutch anti-chauvinism shocks and irritates me tremendously.' (Argentine)

Although in recent years the admiration for world champions and the like has greatly increased, there is more than a grain of truth in the Argentinian's observation. In the Netherlands, pride in one's own nation and culture was rarely strongly developed nor greatly stimulated by government, schools or the media. Only in the face of foreign animosity was this different, e.g. during the Nazi occupation. Even without being part of the resistance, people hid the national flag with love, were moved to tears by the voice of the Queen broadcast from her London exile, secretly wore orange to express (forbidden) royalism, etc.

After the war identification with one's own peer group took over again. Nowadays, many people don't know the words of the national anthem, and the flag is not much honoured anymore. You may see cafés unceremoniously decorate their premises with it, and families use it for their private celebrations of birthdays or passed exams.

As a consequence, other nations' display of nationalism are felt to be slightly ridiculous or even outright irritating. The Dutch distrust countries in which the chief-of-state's portrait hangs everywhere, where street slogans boast of national achievements, where school children must sing national hymns or perform flag ceremonies.

Listening to Dutch people grumbling about the imperfections of their society, one might be tempted to think they don't love their country. However, referring to the Argentinian's irritations with 'Dutch anti-chauvinism', remember that in Dutch culture criticism is an indirect expression of concern or appreciation. So complaining about society or talking critically about certain conditions means that people care. Foreigners may not understand this: *'The Netherlands is constantly occupied with making itself smaller than it really is. That is the real 'hollanditis', a virus that has spread quite widely and that affects people in the street, the professor at university and the politician. (....) Self-scoffing is an often practised sport. The economy is the only field in which the Netherlands don't suffer from an inferiority-complex.'* (France)

I would certainly include football in this last sentence, but it is true that the Dutch don't seem to be proud of themselves. (Some might even say that this book is just more evidence to support this idea ...)

Public negligence of culture Yet the Dutch do love their country: they are fond of its nature, proud of its waterworks, they care for its wildlife, its old city centers, its windmills. It is a rather practical love: visible things rather than symbols. Millions are spent on restoring old houses (useful!) and castles, on saving vulnerable patches of forest or swamp, and the money certainly doesn't only come from the government. Visible as they are, foreigners used to more symbolic or verbal expressions of nationalism can easily overlook these examples as expressions of patriotism.

Some countries loudly advertise their cultural heritage, not only abroad, for touristic reasons, but also to their own citizens, in schools and the media, to raise their citizens' awareness and national pride. This almost never happens in Dutch schools and media. The Dutch school system tries to prepare students for today's society, emphasising personal development and social participation rather than facts and figures. In this view, national chauvinism would be out of place in a united Europe, a world striving for peace and justice.

The result is assertive citizens, but with a remarkable lack of self-esteem for their own culture. Literature and arts are no great source of pride to the Dutch. It came rather as a surprise that translated Dutch literature has been quite successful abroad in recent years.

Another example: when in 1996, the Dutch filmmaker Marleen Gorris won an Oscar for her latest film, all Dutch newspapers proudly announced this, but it was immediately remarked that the film had not been greatly appreciated in its first Dutch showing.

The country's rich past and present are often taken for granted. Although the intellectual elite organises successful expositions at home and abroad, the general Dutch public is not strongly interested in the international prestige of Dutch painters, printers, designers, inventors and scholars ranging from the 15th century to the present.

The Dutch government spends only a rather limited budget on foreign publicity for Dutch culture, and it took pressure from the much more language-conscious Flemish to subsidise the promotion of Dutch literature some years ago at the famous international bookfair in Frankfurt, Germany.

This may also explain why foreigners learning to speak Dutch are looked upon rather with (happy) surprise, but not taken very seriously. Most Dutch people prefer to switch to English rather than exercise the patience to wait for the slow beginner's Dutch answer. Many foreigners practising their newly acquired Dutch get frustrated, like this Englishman: *'It is convenient of course that everyone speaks English, but they even answer me in English when I want to use my Dutch. How do they expect me to learn it if they don't give me the chance to practise?'* (Britain)

A few more things should be said about the use of English in the Netherlands. It is on the increase everywhere, in education, in business, in advertising, in everyday life. After decades of exposure to American and British pop music and years of hard-to-translate computer terminology, using English terms while speaking Dutch has become common practice, although regretted by some. Especially in advertising it is intended to evoke an image of cosmopolitanism, of global culture. As the Dutch economy is open to world trade while the local market is small, by using English it is hoped to expand the sales of products. Any official policy against this, like the French government's objections to 'franglais', is not likely to occur. Some years ago, a Dutch education minister even pleaded for greater use of English in Dutch academic education, so as to better link Dutch academia to the Anglophone world.

Egalitarian nationalism   Contrary to the public negligence of official Dutch culture and quite in line with the 'act normal' attitude, the Dutch can be quite chauvinistic when it comes to more mundane achievements. With a bit of luck(?), one may encounter crowds of youngsters waving flags, wearing bizarre orange-coloured outfits, shouting (for once) 'Holland, Holland!' They are most probably celebrating a national football victory. Sports, football in particular, bring out stronger nationalistic feelings in the Dutch than probably any other event, and in recent years this has been stimulated by extensive – and increasingly commercial – media coverage.

Perhaps this illustrates something new in Dutch society: increasing nationalism. In the 1980s, one TV station started playing the national anthem and showing the flag at the end of the programme. Totally normal in other countries, it raised eyebrows in the Netherlands. Later, other stations copied this, but they are still the exception. Nationalism in the Netherlands is egalitarian: it is best accepted when spontaneously expressed by 'the people', not officially by the state, top to bottom.

As mentioned, European unification seems to be leading to increased national self-awareness all over the continent. In the Dutch government and in intellectual newspapers, debate is going on about the country's position in Europe and in the world. Should it turn away from the Atlantic and take a closer look at Germany and beyond? Should it line up with Belgium and Luxembourg, to be better heard as a collective? Should it go on sending soldiers and money for UN peace actions far away?

Those are mostly government considerations. In the meantime, the Dutch public sees the world as a potential holiday destination, while the Dutch business world keeps seeing it as a market. They read and study, learn languages and take cultural preparation courses.

Chapter 8

ON GENDERS AND GENERATIONS

Vrouwenfietsenmakerij, de, 2e Ceramstr 23/hs .....
('Women's bike repair shop',
as listed in Amsterdam telephone directory)

So far we have discussed the 'mainstream' Dutch business world, that is: the culture of largely male, white, Randstad people. But only half the country is male, more than half the population lives outside the Randstad area, and nowadays many people in the Netherlands are not white. It is time for some moderation of the general picture presented in the previous chapters.

Working in the Netherlands, one will encounter women everywhere and at all times, but not often in managerial positions. Of course, there are exceptions, but usually the women one meets in business are in the mid-level and administrative jobs. The same is true for government positions. Only in healthcare, education and other traditionally 'female' jobs are women over-represented, yet at managerial levels even there one sees more men than women.

'If I had known about the position of working women, I would never have come to Holland.' (Hungarian woman)

In 1996, the United Nations Development Programme rated the Netherlands no. 11 in the world in the field of women's education and position in society; the rest of Holland's 'human development' indicators rated among the very best of the world (no. 4 in 1996). Although the same percentage of women nowadays follows studies as men, they study for a shorter time and achieve a lower grade. Working women produce only a quarter of the Dutch national income. Holland rated 7th in the field of political power of women.[1]

Women and the labour market   Up to just two decades ago, women's participation in the Dutch labour market was low (1981: 30%, 1996: 43%), and their legal status and income downright old-fashioned. Although the legal aspects have much improved (partly under European pressure), even today their share in the job market is, compared with the other EU member states, merely average. If one considers *married* women, the figure is still the lowest of all (56% versus 78% in Britain, 80% in France, 89% in Germany, 92% in neighbouring Belgium, according to 1994 figures by Eurostat). Most of these jobs are part-time.

On average, Dutch women receive only 77% of their male colleagues' hourly salaries for similar jobs, which is close to the world average of 75% (compare: USA 75%, Australia 91%, Britain 70%, Bangladesh 42%).

This male/female difference no longer springs from legal discrimination. It reflects the average Dutch working woman's younger age and therefore shorter work experience or – if she is older – outdated job experience due to career interruptions for child raising.

Most working women in the Netherlands are either young (of the women younger than 30, with or without partner, but without children 86% works) or if not, preferred not to give up their career. The latter implies that these are mostly the better educated women.

All this is not exactly in line with Holland's generally progressive image. Dutch observers mention various reasons. Virtually all point to the rather poor development of childcare facilities in Holland, but there is more to the story than that.

Given the fact that, until two decades ago, many women did not work outside their homes, child daycare facilities are relatively new. As the Dutch authorities impose strict hygienic, pedagogic and safety standards, it is difficult to start such a centre as a private initiative. The official ones, run by organisations and companies, are therefore limited in number and often overbooked, with long waiting lists.

While this is a major hindrance, it also reflects the fact that Dutch family life (in the sense of the nuclear family) is quite strong. Many people prefer to raise their kids themselves rather than hire other people to do so. Most families dine together, go out together, go on holiday together, usually until the children are about 16 years of age.

As a result, many foreigners find the country positively oriented towards children. With the exception of the larger cities, Dutch society in general is still geared to this traditional kind of family. Dutch salaries are high, allowing most families to live on one income, so housewives are assumed to have time to shop in the daytime. Government organisations' opening hours are often from 9 to 5 only, and until very recently, Dutch shopping hours were mostly 9 to 6. Even now, outside the city centres, many shops are closed at 6 and on Sundays.

This makes foreigners in smaller towns sigh that they can't even spend their money: all is open while they are working, but closed when they're free! Many Dutch people don't seem to mind: after legal shopping hour restrictions were relaxed in July 1996, a majority expressed in street surveys that they did not care for longer opening hours! One month later, most customers in the 'new' hours turned out to be singles and 'double income, no kids' type of people.

The editor of a leading Dutch women's magazine gave an interesting but hard-to-prove additional view on women-without-jobs. According to her, Dutch women are quite contented as housewives because that position has a higher status in Holland than in other countries, after centuries of women running the household in the absence of their sea-faring husbands. House-wives were not only managers of the family but also of the farm or the shop, responsible for income and expenses!

A perhaps more substantial explanation can be found in the Dutch tax system. Dutch taxes are not only high but also 'progressive', meaning that the higher the income, the higher the tax percentage. So, unless a couple makes special financial arrangements, any additional income will be taxed on the higher level. Needless to say this doesn't encourage married women to go find a job.

Of the working married women, only one in seven has a full-time job (14%), again the lowest percentage in Europe. Most work part-time. One can look at this phenomenon in two ways: in a negative sense, they couldn't find a full-time one, or in a positive sense, women choose to keep time free to pay attention to their family. Research found out that in 1997 85% of working women were either content about the number of hours they worked (70%) or would like to work less (15%). Also 8% of married *men* work part-time. The Dutch labour market has the highest percentage of part-time jobs in the Western world, made possible by high wages and relative job security. Recently, the legal right to work part-time was accepted by the Dutch Parliament, not much to the liking of employers who find it difficult to accommodate such employees in the work process.

Luckily for the employers, part-time workers are still the exception. The average worker in Holland is a married man whose wife doesn't have a job of her own or just a part-time one. Yet, in the larger cities, a different impression might emerge. One will see plenty of working women, filled shops during extra opening hours, youngsters eating by themselves at fast food places.

Among the younger generation, especially in the cities, the

phenomenon the Dutch call 'double earners' is increasing by 110,000 couples a year. These people are not always married. Dutch law gives couples living together (unmarried but registered) nearly the same legal status as officially married couples. Especially since the 1960s, many people 'live together', permanently or for several years. The main reason is that they value mutual trust more than any legal binding, especially as long as they don't have children. (In a way this is another example of the Dutch not caring very much about authority, the state, the church.)

Such 'living together couples' (mixed or same sex) can choose to keep their incomes separate for taxation or to join them, depending on both partners' income and on their relationship. Since these people are to be found mostly in the cities and are often better educated than married couples, they earn higher average incomes. Working hard but often having no kids, they also have time to consume, making them an attractive target group for advertising luxury products!

Sexism and emancipated men   The general picture still reflects an under-representation of women in the Dutch labour market and, as a matter of fact, also in politics and other decisive sectors.[2] Many Dutch women, feminist or not, don't like this, talk about it, protest against it. Their protest has effected quite a bit of change in recent decades, but there remains a lot still to be done. As in other countries, there have been campaigns for positive discrimination of women, campaigns for encouraging girls to follow studies in traditionally male fields like technology and mathematics. They have had some effect, women say, but changing laws is one thing and changing attitudes another. Sexism exists in the Netherlands, too. Working women, Dutch and foreign, complain of men's subtle discrimination or open harassment.

'Only here I found out about women's problems. In Turkey I never felt second-rank, there are more female architects, doctors and engineers in Turkey than in Holland. It is strange to suddenly realise that here women are treated as "less clever".' (Turkey)

Legal and practical measures have been taken against open harassment, but the more subtle negative attitudes are hard to change. Especially in the more technical branches the older generation of men still tend to 'joke' about women, overlook female talents ('political correctness' is less of an issue in Dutch society than for instance in the USA). By not appreciating women's talents these men, and companies, lose out according to this Argentinian (male) observer: *'The personality of Holland is female. Women here are more intelligent, more attractive, better looking, stronger, more powerful than men. I admire them very much. They are better managers, they will give you an honest answer, you can trust them.'* (Argentine)

Foreigners also observe that Dutch men are quite emancipated: one may see men shopping for food, carrying babies on their back, pushing prams, take their kids for a walk. Especially among the urban well-educated 'double earners', men do part of the household chores: quite a few regularly cook dinners, some do a bit of the cleaning jobs.[3]

'It is surprising to see so many men do the domestic tasks.' (Philippines).

This is all very well, but as long as it isn't 50% of the job, things could improve. Foreign opinions, of course, reflect the observer's own background: *'Women in Dutch society depend too much on the men.'* (Denmark)

'I prefer Dutch men to Irish men. They are more independent. They tell you more, I like that. They are more prepared to listen to you.' (Ireland)

'Here I have freedom. It is perfectly normal for a married woman to have friends of her own, to go dining somewhere without your husband. You can do what you like here. We don't have children, although we've been married for four years. In my country everybody wants to know why not. They think I'm crazy, everyone there has two children because that's the way it should be. Luckily here they don't.' (Czech Republic)

Children and youngsters Although not directly related to business, we want to say something more about children and age in general, because so many visitors, especially from Africa and Asia, wonder: *'Where are the children?'* or *'How come I see so many old people?'* Dutch birth rates are low. It is known that with increasing development, birth rates decline. Children are not needed for extra income and not to care for their parents when they grow old, so with low child mortality rates, just a few children 'will do'.

This is a quite recent phenomenon, however. Holland's population rose very fast in the past few decades, from just 8 million around 1920 to 12 in the 1960s, to 15.5 nowadays. From the 1970s onward, however, the average Dutch family has had just two children. On the other hand, many people don't live in traditional families, they live together or alone: again, especially in cities. Moreover, a large share of the birth rate is taken up by children of ethnic groups, reflecting their still more traditional lifestyles. In large areas of cities like Amsterdam, school classes have mostly or even exclusively 'ethnic' children in them (see chapter 10).

Some observers are outright pessimistic about the younger generations in the Netherlands: *'Young people here don't know what to choose, what to fight for. A large percentage of youngsters is a bit at a loss, studies finished, unemployed, they will just wait and see what happens next. Some join extreme rightist groups, unfortunately. I find that very alarming, who knows where this may lead?'* (Chile)

This is clearly someone concerned about Dutch freedoms and pluriformity, and the effects of the social benefit system. Although many Dutchmen might share his opinion, there is also another view, both from the Dutch and from foreigners: *'Dutch youngsters love challenge. If I have a technical problem, they rush in to solve it. Everybody has good ideas. But they lose interest when a solution is found. In fact, you should give them something new everyday, because they don't like routine.'* (Morocco)

In my opinion, this quotation relates to the more market-oriented and flexible spirit that developed among the young in recent years. Obviously, to compete successfully in the job market, people need a good education, so the Dutch learn and learn. On average, people study up to the age of 18, but many study longer. The Chilean's observation seems to point at another segment of society, the youngsters from the working classes. It also sounds very much like an observation made in one of the larger cities.

All in all, Dutch youngsters are concerned about their future, but not really worried. They feel that if they study and work hard enough, it should be possible to find a satisfactory position in society. In surveys it was revealed that Dutch youngsters find, besides money, personal growth, a good atmosphere and friendly relations with colleagues also important.

Older people With low birth rates and good health care, Dutch society has more old people than young ones. The 'greying' of Holland is under way. Moreover, Dutch people grow very old, they have the longest (average) life expectancy of all: women may reach 80 years old, men a few years less.

Linking this back to business, it means that Holland is not the best market for children's products (although the young share in the general prosperity and have a lot of money to spend!), but a very good and increasing market for the needs of older people.

It means a general restructuring: slowly decreasing needs for education, increasing demand for specialised health care, recreation facilities and consumer products. Problems may arise with financing the needs of large retired groups through the taxation of a decreasing working population. Already, government and financial institutions are pressuring people to save private funds rather than depend on state pensions.

Problems are foreseen for the years after 2010, when the 'post war baby boom' will reach pensioning age. But then, what is 'the pension age'? Officially it is 65, but: *'I have the impression that virtually nobody here works until the age of sixty five.'* (USA)

The observation is correct to some degree. Many people take early retirement, through private savings, special arrangements with their insurance company or accepting freedom-with-less-money. The pension age of government workers has been made flexible, and in companies, too, things can be arranged, although at considerable cost for the person involved. With the 'greying' of Holland, employers are calling for people to work *longer* than the age of 65, rather than retire early.

Once people retire, they can still enjoy a pleasant life for years, given the long lives most Dutchmen can expect. For the really elderly, there are good provisions, like in many other Western countries, but foreigners do not always understand: *'I was extremely shocked to find that this (Dutch) family I visited had sent their own mother to a home for the aged, while having a dog sit on the sofa as if it were a family member.'* (Tanzania)

Quoting this to Dutchmen, they will look up with smiling surprise at first and then agree that it must look strange.

'It is strange that the concept of family here has such a limited meaning. Family here, that is Dad, Mum, brother, sister, sometimes Grandpa and Grandma, but that's it.' (Cameroon)

The average Dutch family is indeed nuclear, Dad, Mum and the children. Most Dutch children have a lot of freedom, their own room, their own music, their own TV set quite often. But houses are not large, so grandparents often prefer to stay in their own home as long as possible, not bothering their (hard working) children, nor being bothered by rock music.

If bad health requires more intensive assistance than relatives can provide, there are organisations that supply meals, cleaning and basic medical help. For the worst cases, there are special quiet homes for the elderly, providing full care, including recreational and medical facilities.

Although old people may prefer this themselves, even to other Westerners it may come as a bit of a shock: *'The Dutch have lost the contact between the generations. You never see a grandmother here living with her daughter or son. Older people are put away somewhere, there is no more family feeling.'* (Ireland)

Individualism and hospitality   Of course, there are sad circumstances sometimes, e.g. for old people without children. Unfortunately, the following observations are true: *'There are many people here who feel alone. You read more and more about elderly people found dead in their home. When recently I heard about a woman who gets money just to visit an old lady, I was happy to be Turkish. With us that is different.'* (Turkey)

'People are nice here, but they don't make an effort to get in touch with you. They leave you alone too much. In the apartment where I live, they helped me when I locked myself out, but afterwards they were at a distance again.' (South Africa)

Yes, Dutch society, like other Western cultures, is 'atomising': individualism is important, and it shocks people from more 'collectivist' cultures. Especially in larger cities, many people live alone. More than 50% of all households there consist of just one person (single, divorced or widowed). Now, living alone is not always the same as loneliness, but that may be hard to see for foreigners. Exactly like their married counterparts, these people have their friends and colleagues, their hobbies or sports clubs, their theatre visits, etc. This implies that even the single Dutch person's leisure time is often highly structured, not by the family, but by the 8 o'clock start of the above activities. Small wonder this observation was made: *'It is very hard to get your Dutch colleagues to go for a beer after work, I at least didn't succeed in that yet.'* (Finland)

One-person households have their consequences for 'the market': the number of households obviously increases (each needing their own refrigerator, etc.), and more and more small one-person portions of food and other products are sold. When marketing or selling in Holland, business people might like to keep this in mind.

One last aspect of individualism affects foreign visitors and should be mentioned therefore. Dutch people being so individualistic, they assume that everyone is also like that and prefers to be left alone, free to make their own choices, to do as they like (the Dutch word for hospitality, *gastvrijheid*, literally translates as guest-freedom!). So foreign colleagues, trainees, business visitors are not always offered the kind of hospitality that they themselves might extend to guests at home.

In the Netherlands, invitations are given for set evenings or weekends. Then the Dutch hosts will cook their best food, lay the table nicely, select music to please them, take them out to a place that might interest the visitor, etc. The guests receive all the family's attention and anyone dropping in or phoning will be kept away. However, this shower of attention lasts only as long as that particular dinner party, that particular one-day excursion. Western visitors have few problems with it: *'I always found Dutchmen very hospitable. Allright, you must make an arrangement to visit them and I had to get used to that. But once the arrangement is made, they receive you very well.'* (Iceland)

But a woman from India commented: *'In India we had Dutch expatriates for neighbours. We went to their house to say hallo, welcomed them with a dinner party and offered our help. When we moved to Holland, we expected the same in reverse, but nobody came. I had to go and ask them in. Then only they came. That was very disappointing to us, but I must add that later they were very nice to us.'*

Privacy is a major concept in Dutch culture. Neighbours don't like to intrude upon people who are still cleaning up their things, ordering their furniture, setting up household. Remember the paragraphs on charity: the Dutch are sensitive to anyone who needs help, but they also respect people's privacy, so help is almost always given, but only if asked for.

Thus, the Dutch think of themselves as very hospitable, doing their best to please their guests. But given their sense of privacy, their many private activities and their family orientation, Dutch hospitality does not imply a non-stop welcome to the house at any given time; it is restricted. To people from countries where the door is always open for anyone to drop in, this is disappointing: *'People here are different, more business-like. I have only once visited a Dutch home, for reasons of work, but never for just a cup of tea.'* (Egypt)

All this is rather different in more rural, less individualised parts of the country away from the Randstad area, where community feelings are (still) stronger. Let us explore the regional varieties of the Netherlands.

1. Figures mentioned in this chapter were found in various articles in the NRC-Handels-blad newspaper of 1995, 1996 and 1997.

2. Some figures for 1995: men/women participation in the labour market: 85%/43%; entrepreneurs male/female: 76.6%/23.4%; managers male/female: 83.8%/16.2%; professors male/female: 95.8%/4.2%; members of parliament (the Lower House) male/female: 67.3%/32.7%; mayors male/female: 84.8%/15.2%. Total working population male/female 62.6%/37.4%.

3. In 1995 men on average spent 12 hours per week on domestic tasks, women 26 hours.

Chapter 9

REGIONS VERSUS RANDSTAD[1]

Netherlanders and Hollanders:
regional diversity in a small country

There is more to the Netherlands than just 'Holland'. However small the country may be, regionalism is still present nowadays, although geographical mobility is strong. All types of (tele)communication link areas together, and the level of prosperity is more or less the same throughout the country.

People outside the dominant Randstad area feel themselves to be different from 'Holland'. Especially in the northernmost and southernmost provinces (Friesland, Limburg), people object to being called 'Hollanders'. They consider themselves 'Netherlanders' but definitely not Hollanders. To them, the 'real' Hollanders are arrogant, big-mouthed, hurried, overly businesslike and rather too eager for anything modern or non-conformist. Many of the 'real' Hollanders – most of the city-dwellers – proudly agree, in return calling *them* 'provincials', 'peasants': slightly old-fashioned or outright conservatist, somewhat naive, slow-minded.

The dominance of the west developed after the 1500s, when the sea-faring trade developed. Holland proper gradually overruled the Hanseatic river trading network in which eastern river cities like Kampen, Deventer and Zutphen had flourished.

Regionalism Regionalism was institutionalised in the federal character of the Dutch republic. It wasn't until 1813 that a unified state came into existence, but it took modernisations like railways and bridges to initiate a truly 'psychological' unification, a sense of 'Dutchness' for all. In recent decades, modern media on a national scale has accelerated this process, as has the growing labour mobility. But even now, regionalism survives in jokes and opinions about people from other areas, in competitive feelings between regions, in fierce allegiance to local sports clubs.

Local dialects are strong in many areas, and Dutchmen can often tell when people are from outside their area, if not always their exact origin. Until some decades ago, speaking a dialect was frowned upon in schools. Even nowadays it is considered not very 'classy' (in Dutch intellectual and business circles little dialect is heard), and fun is made of strong dialects. In recent years, however, there seems to be a certain resurge of appreciation of dialects, as indicating 'roots' and 'authenticity'. Food products are sometimes advertised with voices speaking dialect, hinting at 'home-made', 'natural' qualities. Pop music in provincial dialects now thrives among the younger generation, even outside the area from which the band originates.

Such phenomena may seem odd in the age of globalisation and European integration, but they probably reflect the uncertainty these processes bring about. They could also be interpreted as counterreactions to the dominance of the prosperous, business-like Randstad area or, some say, to the discussion on ethnic identity among the minorities in the country (see next chapter): 'if they are proud of their heritage, well, so are we of ours!'

Generally speaking, *northerners* and *easterners* are felt to be less outspoken but more sociable than people from the dominant Randstad area. They have a reputation of being more introverted, not using many words if something can be said with just a few. This might reflect their less intensive exposure to the speedy and business-like pace of life in late 20th century society, and to foreign contacts.

In contrast, *southerners* are felt to be more outgoing, enjoying life's pleasures more, taking more time for personal affairs. They are also slightly less individualistic and more oriented towards relatives and people from their hometown. Finally, they are also felt to be less egalitarian, more hierarchic, more respectful of authorities like the boss, the bishop and political figures. Both outsiders and the southerners themselves point out that all this is related to the fact that 'the South' – the part of the Netherlands which lies south of the 'big rivers' (Rhine, Waal and Maas), except for the province of Zeeland – was never Calvinistic. It remained Catholic when the rest of the country turned Protestant. Again, some of these perceptions may be stereotypes, but there is a grain of truth present. Let's look in more detail at a survey of the country from north to south.

Friesland (610,000 inhabitants)   To the Dutch this northern province evokes an image of milk and cows, lakes, ice-skating, sailing with dark-sailed ships, quaint old villages on man-made elevations *(terpen)*. Frisians bear a certain resemblance to the Vikings: stereotypically blond-haired, speaking among themselves their own language (Fries or as they say Frysk, a separate branch of the Germanic language family). They are the descendants of tribes described by the Romans as fierce warriors, and they are still perceived to be sturdy and stubborn. They are said to be hard-working and, once you have gained their trust, very loyal, but watch out: they also have a touch of anti-authoritarianism and, if provoked, easily lose their temper! In the past century this stimulated some strong socialist and even anarchistic political movements in Friesland.

It is a fertile area, but for many centuries it was a low-lying near-peninsula threatened by strong gales. Farmers and fishermen here always successfully kept feudal overlords at bay, gaining them 'Frisian Freedom'. Until recently, Friesland was a mostly agricultural area, lending its name to the typical black-and-white cows. In recent decades, a large and worldwide exporting dairy industry (Friesland Dairy Products) developed out of former cooperatives. Some other industries (Philips, Fokker) also settled in the province. Tourism to the islands – which each have their own identity and mentality! – and to the lakes is another source of provincial income.

Even today, regionalism is quite strong in Friesland, with a drive for cultural autonomy: local media are popular, and as of 1996 the name of the province was officially changed to *Fryslân*. Towns have names in both dialect and Dutch, and primary education is partly in the Frisian language. Friesland also boasts the country's strongest folkloristic traditions (costumes, handi-craft, special sports). In very cold winters it organises the longest 'official' ice-skating tour of the country, attracting thousands of participants. This 220 km long 'Eleven Cities Tour' was held in 1986 and then again in 1997.

Groningen (560,000 inhabitants)   The province where enorm-ous quantities of natural gas have been exploited since 1960 by the parastate organisation GasUnie, which provides not only all of the Netherlands but large parts of Western Europe with high quality gas. Culturally, Groningen enjoys a less distinctive image than Friesland. Groningen city (the sixth largest in the country) lies about 2 to 3 hours travelling northeast from the Randstad. In a small country this is felt to be distant, and westerners perceive Groningen as almost 'Scandinavian'. Its liveliness is, therefore, somewhat unexpected, mostly due to its character as a university town and the northern cultural and economic capital. By government order of the 1980s, Groningen houses the large, now privatised Dutch telecommunications organisation KPN. Still the province would like more investments, promoting its space and quality of life with a hint to its northernmost position on the map: 'There is nothing above Groningen!'

Drenthe (460,000 inhabitants) Sand, moors, woods and archae-ological remains form its image. Up to the 20th century it was a poor, thinly populated and quite isolated area of infertile sandy soils. Even in the 1920s people still harvested peat under con-ditions which are hardly believable just 70 years later. People here are known to be quiet and introverted. Yet many Dutch tourists visit this province for its age-old rock-graves and beautiful nature. South of Emmen, some oil was exploited by Shell.

Overijssel and Gelderland   Overijssel (1,060,000 inhabitants) and Gelderland (1,880,000 inhabitants) are two provinces with less outspoken images, although their wooded and hilly areas are popular for holidays and as a living environment. The eastern part of Overijssel, called Twente, still suffers from the breakdown of its textile industry in the 1960s. What has remained are a strong machine industry and a technical university. It has perhaps the strongest regional identity. People there are nicknamed 'Tukkers', and their reputation resembles that of Drenthe people: silent and somewhat closed to outsiders.

Several towns along the IJssel river were medieval trading centres, with attractive old town centres. Arnhem and Nijmegen lie close to Germany, with modern city centres, rebuilt after extensive war damage. These cities link the Randstad area to the industrial Ruhrgebiet in Germany. Economic activity is very varied. It ranges from various kinds of manufacturing to national and regional services (Nijmegen Catholic University).

The Gelderland river area called Betuwe received international press coverage in 1995, when a threat of flooding required the evacuation of more than 200,000 people and all of the cattle.

The Bible Belt   The western edges of Overijssel and Gelderland (the Veluwe area), the eastern and southern rural parts of Utrecht, Zuid-Holland and much of the island province of Zeeland are part of what could be described as 'the Dutch Bible Belt': an area stretching diagonally from northern Overijssel southwestwards to Zeeland. This rural area has a high proportion of orthodox Calvinists. Economically, these 250,000 people are mostly involved in farming, local shops, small construction work and manufacturing. Some of them, like the people of the former island Urk, are fishermen. Their social life is still strongly dictated by fundamentalist interpretations of the Bible: frequent church attendance and absolute observance of Sunday as a day without work. Both insurance and vaccinations may be considered as opposing God's will, and abhor the modern aspects of city life, including television. On the basis of different Bible inter-pretations (hard to follow for outsiders), this group is subdivided into various denominations, political parties and related institutions like schools, etc. Referring to their stern way of clothing, other Dutchmen nickname them 'black stocking churches'. One such party decided in 1995 that women could vote but not represent them in political bodies, and most women and girls of that group agreed.

Flevoland   Before turning to the south, something should be said about the newest province of the Netherlands, Flevoland (280,000 inhabitants). Newest? Yes, this province was officially inaugurated only in 1985. Before 1940 the area was the Zuiderzee, a large body of water in the heart of the country, with two tiny islands. After devastating floods in 1916, it was decided that it should be closed off and partially reclaimed. Flevoland is the result of decades of hard work by thousands of people, managed by a powerful government body. It is a 'hightech' province of straight lines. Modern farms are run by 'immigrant' farmers from the northern provinces, while two planned towns (Lelystad and Almere) provide housing for city people from the overcrowded Randstad area. So far, only small-scale industry and companies in the service sector have followed.

Obviously, cultural identity and natural beauty cannot grow in a short time, so the area tends to be overlooked by the Dutch. Yet the province boasts several attractions, also for foreigners: *'This is incredible! Isn't it amazing to realise that all of this is not just nature but man-made land!'* (USA)

Now let us turn south.

Zeeland (370,000 inhabitants)   As the name implies, a province with many water-related connotations: islands, waterways, huge dams and bridges, beaches, oysters and mussels. It also boasts beautiful towns, traditional costumes and various island dialects. Until the construction of giant sea-dams after the 1953 flood disaster, this island province was not only isolated from the rest of the country but also internally, which explains the differences between the islands and villages, and also the low population density.

Due to its close proximity to Britain, trade between the two countries has existed since Roman times, while in the 17th century Zeeland's seafarers were among the Dutch explorers and conquerors of the Pacific (*New* Zealand!). In some Caribbean villages, descendants of slaves even in this century still spoke a kind of pidgin Zeeland dialect.

Although Zeeland still has a rural image, the port of Vlissingen is an industrial area, with a nuclear power plant nearby. Its harbour profits from the spill off from Rotterdam, and from being an outpost to Belgium's main port Antwerp.

The southernmost part of the province, Zeeuws-Vlaanderen (Zeeland Flanders), can only be reached (from Holland) by ferry, but a tunnel/bridge connection will be completed in 2002. Here one finds the industrial area of Terneuzen, where Akzo Chemicals has a huge plant. The area links up with Belgian industry along the canal connecting the city of Gent (Gand) to the sea through Dutch territory.

That Zeeland suffered from regular flooding was never much noticed elsewhere because of its relative isolation. Only after the devastating flood of 1953, in which more than 1800 people drowned, did the rest of the country realise that something should be done. The Delta Plan was soon started, a complex of huge and ingenious dams blocking the sea out from between the islands and connecting these to the mainland. It changed the character of the communities there, even before the final dam was closed in 1985, as Dutch and later also German tourists discovered the beauty of the islands, and as people from Zeeland started commuting to work in the Rotterdam harbour area.

Noord-Brabant[2] (2,290,000 inhabitants)   To the Dutch, this province evokes images of sand and woods, with a slightly Latin atmosphere that includes carnival feasting in February, and large and sociable families enjoying food and drinks, but also of Van Gogh and, more up-to-date, of Philips lamps. It is the most industrialised province and densely inhabited. The image reflects its past, a feudal society of rich and noble families owning sandy and infertile land worked by poor peasants. Villages had a clear hierarchy, with land owner, church pastor and a few other 'notables' exercising control. Some of this still lingers, although nowadays 'immigration' from other provinces blurs this picture.

Together with Limburg, Brabant remained Catholic during and after the Reformation. Both provinces were occupied by troops of the Dutch republic in the war against Spain (1568-1648), and were always governed directly from The Hague. Political representation first appeared after the 1795 revolution. Brabant being closer to the Randstad than Limburg, it is nowadays fully incorporated into the rest of the country.

In the late 19th century, the northern Philips family invested in the then poor, low wage area of Eindhoven to set up a factory of electric lamps. It made Eindhoven the fifth largest city of the Netherlands. Even today it is still the city of Philips. Nearby there is also the DAF truck factory. Tilburg, once a textile town, has a university and houses Fuji, one of the major Japanese investments in the Netherlands. Breda and the provincial capital Den Bosch have less distinct economic images.

Regarding the matter of mentality, people from Brabant are known to enjoy life better than northern Calvinists can. Feasting, eating and drinking come to them more naturally, it seems. Possibly as a result of the stricter feudal and Catholic hierarchy, they also have the reputation of being more respectful to authorities, less critical, less blunt. In the business world this may lead to more attention to 'representation': lunches and dinners, dressing up for occasions, slightly more formal manners, taking more time for getting to know each other. Latin, just a bit of it.

Limburg   This feeling is even stronger with people from the last province dealt with here Limburg (1,140,000 inhabitants). The extreme southeastern location and the strange oblong shape of this province suggest a special position in the country. Visiting it, one indeed notes that its character is rather un-Dutch, especially in the south: rolling hills (part of the Belgian Ardennes), another type of farms and villages, a distinctly different lifestyle. Among themselves, Limburgers speak a strong dialect, barely understandable for northern listeners. Its most distinctive feature is the so-called 'soft G' (also heard in Noord-Brabant), a rather more charming way of pronouncing this letter than in official Dutch. Northerners may hear this with a mixture of jealousy and superiority feelings, the latter based on the oldtime low status of Catholic areas occupied by the Protestant north.

Limburg's capital city of Maastricht, now internationally famous for the European Union treaty, can be called the most Latin city of the Netherlands: well-dressed people, luxury shops, outstanding restaurants. Limburg hints at all this un-Dutchness in tourist advertisements up north: 'Come visit our own foreign land'. The northerners happily follow this advice.

Quite another kind of Limburg lies close by: an area of coal mines closed in the 1960s, when Groningen's discovery of natural gas made coal unremunerative. The large chemical industry DSM used to be the state mining company. The Dutch government tried to counteract another consequence of the closed mines, unemployment, by relocating the headquarters of the former Dutch state pension fund ABP from The Hague to the southeastern city of Heerlen. Quite a few of the younger miners found new employment after Volvo-Mitsubishi investments (Nedcar) in the previously Dutch passengercar industry DAF, at Born near Sittard. The mid-Limburg city of Venlo is a cargo traffic centre serving all of Europe and the hometown of Océ, one of the world's leading companies in photocopiers. Limburg advocates its 'Euregion' character, with German and Belgian industries nearby, to attract foreign business people and other visitors.

Limburg's business culture approaches southern European ways: less down-to-earth behaviour, a bit more ceremony, more time for initial contact, less outspoken criticism, more chances of being invited out to lunch or dine. But northerners might add: also some less correct business practices, after a few such incidents were publicised exhaustively in the national and regional press.

What causes this province to be so different from the rest of the country? Well, Limburg might easily have become Belgian or German had history taken a slightly different turn. In fact, the adjoining Belgian province is also named Limburg. The original province was divided in two more or less equal parts after Belgium became a separate country in 1830. Up to the 1920s there were Limburgers (peacefully) striving to join Belgium!

Most Limburgers now feel quite content with being Dutch. The rest of the country happily allows them to remain slightly different. Even a few foreigners do: '*Sometimes I go to Maastricht. It is more formal there than in Amsterdam, but I like being there. People are happier, more open, they are not Calvinistic. I feel related to them. Calvinists are even more religious and stern than the Irish.*' (Ireland)

Randstad   So all of this is *not* the Randstad. Thus, the foreigner might still wonder, what then *is* the Randstad? The introductory chapter mentioned how the Randstad is the dominant area of the country. Here we will add something about its geographical and cultural structure.

The word Randstad, meaning 'ring-city' or 'edge-city', was invented not so long ago for the cluster of cities in the west which encircle a rather empty agricultural area in the provinces of Noord-Holland (2.5 million), Zuid-Holland (3.4 million) and Utrecht (1.1 million). There are four main centres in this 'ring-city': Rotterdam (agglomeration: 1.1 million inhabitants), The Hague (700,000), Amsterdam (1.1 million) and Utrecht (550,000). Taken together, these cities and the adjoining towns and villages are a metropolis of more than six million people. With its economic and cultural activities, living there is attractive to many, so further growth is expected. Travelling through the Randstad, foreigners may see it as one large conglomeration, but only in recent years, with increasing mobility, has a kind of shared urban identity grown up. Individual cities (and even villages) still boast their own dialect, mentality, history, traditions, culture. Here is an overview, starting in the south.

Dordrecht: a quiet old town, famous for its 17th century role in Calvinism and later as the centre of the regional shipping and metal industry.

Rotterdam: the busy economic heart of the country is the most modern Dutch city, being continuously rebuilt ever since the 1940 Nazi bombings destroyed the old centre. Rotterdam is home to many important economic and scientific activities like Unilever and Erasmus University. Its port areas (Europoort, Maasvlakte) stretch for over 30 km to the sea and house shipping and shipping-related companies, oil refineries, and Europe's largest cargo storage. In fact, Rotterdam is the main harbour for the German Ruhrgebiet, with which it is connected by an excellent inland waterway, the Rhine. In terms of mentality, its inhabitants are known to be hardworking, money-minded and somewhat chauvinistic, especially about their famous Feyenoord football club. Towns like Vlaardingen and Schiedam are part of Rotterdam's conurbation.

Delft: a quaint historical town, but also home to one of the world's most famous technical universities, and to Gist-Brocades chemical research and food industry.

The Hague (Den Haag in Dutch): the political capital, housing the Queen, Parliament, ministries, foreign embassies and the International Court of Justice. Royal Dutch Shell's headquarters is also there, and numerous national organisations. In spite of its size and many activities, it has remained a pleasant, quiet, green city, where many foreign expatriates choose to live. Other Dutchmen do not always appreciate the Hagueners' slightly formal living styles.

Leiden: another historical and industrial town, home to the country's oldest university (1574), with a very prestigious law department.

Haarlem: even more history, and Holland's largest international printing company Enschedé that produces not only Dutch money, passports and the like, but also those of many foreign countries. Many wealthy Dutch families live in Haarlem's green suburbs, close to the sea.

Schiphol/Hoofddorp: the area where the international airport of Amsterdam is situated, was until the 1860s a dangerous lake. The lake changed into fertile farmland in the 1870/80s and part of it became the airport of Schiphol after World War I. Schiphol and the adjacent Hoofddorp now are a rapidly growing conglomeration around Europe's fourth busiest airport, 'The gateway to Europe' (lying below sea level), with offices (KLM and many others) and industries related to air traffic and digital communication.

Amsterdam: the official capital and self-appointed cultural centre of the country. With its long history of cosmopolitanism and civic freedom, it houses the hub of Holland's cultural elite and is home to scores of non-conformists. Its canals, theatres, museums and nightlife and its very liberal atmosphere attract millions of tourists each year. Some may find it a bit too exciting, but the locals (including much 'import') are fiercely chauvinistic about their city's avant-garde position, its mixed reputation and of course its football team Ajax. Amsterdammers are the most extroverted northerners. Their well-known humour and dialect (mostly restricted to working class people) still reflect the former Jewish subculture of the city. All this might make people forget that Amsterdam is also home to the Dutch stock market, many Dutch and international banks (ABN-Amro, ING), two universities, the diamond industry and several graphic industries, including some national newspapers. Its port, still important after four centuries, is linked by a large canal to the North Sea at the town of IJmuiden, where one finds the Dutch blast furnaces and steel factories of Hoogovens.

Zaanstad: in the 17th century the villages along the river Zaan became one of the most important staple markets for products from the Baltic and tropical areas. Out of industries related to this function and to shipbuilding and sailing grew several modern ones, like Ahold (food and supermarkets), Verkade (chocolate) and the linoleum/carpet industry.

Hilversum (and other towns in the Gooi region): the Dutch radio and TV capital. For the rest a quiet residential green city.

Utrecht: the fourth city of the country and 2000 years old. It is the Dutch railway hub (including its headquarters), boasts the country's largest exposition and fair grounds and its largest shopping mall. Utrecht is also the traditional capital of the Dutch Catholic church and some other denominations. Its large student population (the largest university is located there) has changed the outdated reputation of Utrechters as being somewhat introverted and 'stiff'.

Green Heart   Finally the areas in between, the so-called *Green Heart,* and the surrounding parts of the two Holland provinces. These are still relatively empty regions with, until recently, a mostly agricultural orientation: green pastures with cows, straight ditches and meandering rivers, old farms and quaint villages and towns like Gouda and Woerden. But the area is under heavy pressure from the surrounding cities and their surplus population. Some villages like Zoetermeer and Alphen aan de Rijn have grown into towns with modern suburbs. Schiphol Airport is eating away empty space, while new motorways and railway connections (including a high-speed one) threaten to disturb the rural calm, and dense traffic creates jams all around the cities. The inhabitants of the Green Heart worry and protest, while authorities at all levels set rules and regulations to keep things under control. So far, it has worked, more or less, and foreigners can still admire 'typically Dutch' scenes of green meadows, canals, windmills and tulip fields. Yet it remains uncertain how much of it can be saved from urbanisation and economic pressure.

1. Population figures in this chapter are from CBS, *Statistisch Jaarboek* 1997, and concern the year 1996.

2. Noord means 'North'. South-Brabant is the Belgian province of Brabant, around Brussels. Confusingly, many Dutch people also simply refer to Noord-Brabant as 'Brabant'.

Chapter 10

ON ETHNIC VARIETY

'What the farmer doesn't know, he won't eat'
(Old Dutch saying)

Visiting business people and expatriates to the Netherlands cannot fail to notice that they are definitely not the only foreigners there. In this chapter, we focus on people of non-Dutch origin who are permanently residing in the Netherlands, not on temporary expatriates.

Much more controversial than regional variety is the presence of ethnic minorities and other foreign groups in the Netherlands. Estimates are that some 10% of the present population of 15.5 million[1] was not born here, or (at least one of) their parents were not (excluded in this figure are people from other European. Union member states). About half of them are people from former Dutch colonies, who had Dutch citizenship to start with.

The position of minorities and the arrival of more immigrants are under sometimes fierce debate, in Parliament, in the streets and in living rooms. Before going into more detail, let us indicate the importance of this chapter to the foreign reader intending to come to Holland for work.

Immigrants Working in the Netherlands, one cannot fail to notice these immigrants (or their children), although one may not always recognise them by their looks. About half of the four main minorities lives in the four major Randstad cities. In these cities ethnic minorities make up 25% of the total population, and up to 39% if all persons born outside the Netherlands or with at least one of their parents born in another country are included. As elsewhere in Western Europe, immigrants (unlike expatriates) are found more in the lower levels of society and of business, but there are exceptions, depending for example on the history of the individual's group. Immigrants' jobs range from simple work like cleaning to shop keepers to secretaries to – occasionally – managerial posts. Upward social mobility has started among most groups.

Of course, it is impossible to generalise about their vastly different cultural characteristics. Yet, by contrasting them to 'native' Dutchmen, one might say that these groups share some values: more relation-oriented, stronger family ties, often more religious, and – also related to their minority status – a stronger sense of belonging to a group.

Not sharing the typically Dutch backgrounds described in

previous chapters, they may come across as less 'brutally honest', less overtly critical, less impatient than the Dutch in their dealings with people and business. Having said this, let's now look at some of the major groups, and the general position of 'foreigners' in Dutch society.

The Netherlands never perceived itself as an official 'immigration country' up to the 1970s. Some immigration of Iberian *Jews* and French *Huguenots* occurred long ago, immediately after the Dutch Republic granted people religious freedom. Later, in the 1930s, a group of *Chinese* found shelter in Holland when the Dutch shipping companies they had worked for suffered from the severe economic crisis. But these arrivals were felt to have been unique historical events.

In fact, there was quite some migration *from* Holland after the Second World War. Some 300,000 Dutchmen started a new life in Australia, New Zealand, South Africa, Canada and the USA during the bleak post-war years, when the Cold War threw uncomfortable shadows over Europe.

People from the former Dutch East Indies   Almost at the same time people started arriving from the former colony of *Indonesia*, where the struggle for independence made life difficult not only for Dutch colonials (just liberated from Japanese camps) but also for local people working for the colonial authorities. Some 200,000 people arrived from the former 'Dutch East Indies', many of them in Europe for the first time, and quite a few of them with some degree of Indonesian looks and habits. They received little attention and no privileges whatsoever at a time when the Dutch were working hard to overcome their own economic and psychological war damage. Often well educated and speaking perfect Dutch, all of them silently and successfully integrated into Dutch society.

Among them was a distinct category that later caused some political violence in Holland: the *South Moluccans*, a group of colonial military personnel (and their families) from the East Indonesian archipelago. They had faithfully served the Dutch for centuries, most having converted to Christianity in the process. They had been promised regional autonomy or even independence by the Dutch, but Indonesia developed a centralised system without such arrangements. Their former employers could do little more than ship them to Holland, temporarily it was thought then. As the years went by, their dream of independence was revealed to be an illusion, and their refugee camps became permanent settlements. The first generation of obedient soldiers grew old in patient silence, but their children learned to speak better Dutch and express themselves in society. Moluccan youngsters occupied the Indonesian embassy and hijacked Dutch trains in the 1970s, trying to force Indonesia into granting autonomy to their never-seen islands after all. It cost some human life and caused great upheaval in politically non-violent Holland.

All the Dutch government could do was tactfully plead their case with Indonesia, with no more result than that the few people who wished to do so were allowed to return in peace. Nearly all stayed in Holland, many of them intermarrying, others mixing more with the Dutch.

People from the (former) Dutch West Indies   A second wave of post-colonial immigration occurred in the mid-1970s. The Dutch colony of *Surinam*, in South America, had been granted independence in 1975, after 20 years of an autonomous status within the Kingdom. Its population of 400,000 consisted mainly of two roughly equal groups of different ethnic backgrounds. One was of black African origin, descendants of the plantation slaves liberated in 1863. The other was of Indian origin, descendants of migrated Hindustani workers who had replaced those liberated slaves on the plantations. Both groups had organised themselves politically, and at independence each feared that the other group would seize power and oppress them. All had Dutch passports, all had been taught to see Holland as a kind of superior paradise, so many preferred far-away security over insecurity at home.

Between 1970 and 1975, some 150,000 people quite unexpectedly arrived in Holland, causing immediate problems with housing, work and schooling for their children. In Amsterdam a new suburb turned into an 'immigrant area' rather than into the luxury middle class area as planned. (When in 1992 a crashing airplane there killed 56 people from various ethnicities, a multicultural and multireligious ceremony impressed millions of TV viewers all over the country.)

The Surinamese advantage over the 'guest workers' (see below) was that they could speak Dutch, but their educational level was not always geared to the by now sophisticated Dutch economy. After considerable initial problems, however, their integration was not unsuccessful. After 1980, military dictatorship and economic upheaval in independent Suriname kept them in the Netherlands. The military coup even caused a new wave of immigrants. With their relatives following to join them, the group numbers now some 290,000 people, virtually all of whom are Dutch citizens. Most of them have established a considerable degree of socio-cultural integration, and quite a few have achieved good positions in Dutch society.

Another group of ex-colonial citizens arrived less conspicuously. Five islands in the Caribbean are called 'The Netherlands Antilles'. They and the politically separate island of *Aruba* are semi-independent parts of the Kingdom of the Netherlands, altogether home to some 300,000 people. In the larger islands near Venezuela, people speak 'Papiamento', a pidgin language resembling Spanish, while in the smaller ones east of Puerto Rico, English is spoken. All inhabitants learn Dutch in school.

Due to the frequently unfavourable economic conditions in the islands, and again to the Eldorado image of the 'motherland', many inhabitants chose to come to Holland, amounting to some 96,700 in 1996. Arriving in small groups and, like the Surinamese, speaking Dutch more or less fluently, there was never any great publicity surrounding them. Perhaps that is why the Dutch general public ignorantly tends to call them Surinamese as well, somewhat to the Antilleans' dismay.

People from Turkey and Morocco Some ten years before the arrival of the Surinamers, another type of migration began that had nothing to do with the Dutch colonial past. During the 1960s, the Dutch economy boomed, and the Dutch could now afford good and extended education. There was a serious shortage of blue collar workers and, as in surrounding countries, work contracts were given to unskilled labourers from rural communities in less prosperous nations around the Mediterranean, first from Italy, Spain, Greece and Yugoslavia, later *Morocco* and *Turkey*. Young men arrived by the thousands, speaking only their own language, many of them Muslim. Employers and government bodies, assuming they would not stay, did little or nothing to introduce them to Dutch society. They just were put to work, given provisional (and often very poor) housing and left to themselves. The Dutch public also did not pay much attention to them.

The 'guest workers', as they were called, had hoped to earn quick money and send it home to their relatives. But life in Holland was far more expensive than foreseen, and not much could be saved up. If they were lucky, their work contract was prolonged, and they stayed. As their home economies improved, most Spaniards, Greeks and Italians returned home, but the Moroccans and Turks remained. The Dutch government permitted their wives and children to join them, and they came, for the first time out of their rural surroundings into foreign, urbanised Holland. The families often found housing in dilapidated, cheap blocks built during the industrial revolution of the 1880s. Dutch working class people were moving away from such areas to greener suburbs, if they could afford it. In the old neighbourhoods, the immigrants set up shops catering for their needs, organised places for worship and community centres. Gradually, Holland saw the rise of ethnic groups with a totally different culture, living mostly in working class areas just outside the city centre. In 1996 there lived circa 265,000 Turks and circa 225,000 Moroccans in the Netherlands.

Up to the 1980s the Dutch economy generally thrived, and there was little competition with the foreign workers. Then things changed: unemployment rose among the Dutch but more strongly among the foreign workers. Although the immigrants had paid taxes for years, resistance grew to the fact that they could reap the now extensive Dutch social benefits just like anyone else.

At a time when on international television fierce-looking groups violently advocated Islamic revolution, irritations in Holland were voiced more and more openly about the foreigners' cultural habits, their women's scarves, their Muslim beliefs. Both authorities and individuals started worrying about potential ethnic violence. Activities were set up for both integrating the ethnic groups and soothing the locals, but generally speaking it appeared too late to bring the two groups to integrate. As more and more critical or outright racist thoughts were heard in Dutch society, many of the 'allochthonous' people (as they were now called officially, meaning: born elsewhere) clung to their own group and religion for comfort and a sense of belonging.

Refugees   Starting in the 1970s and still continuing, Europe witnessed an increase in the arrival of legal and illegal *refugees* from countries all over the world. Civil wars, political repression, religious prosecution and economic misery cause people to look for a better life in wealthy continents and peaceful countries. In those countries, including the Netherlands, authorities try to distinguish between real *political refugees* and fortune seekers ('economic refugees'). Authorities are under pressure from sections of the public fearing abuse of social benefits, financed by increased taxes, loss of established social peace, religious fanaticism or even, in the Dutch case, more overpopulation. The fact that many refugees request political asylum has earned them the general name '*asylum seekers*'. In the Netherlands, some large groups in this category are people from Somalia, Iran, former Yugoslavia, Ghana and Sri Lanka.

Multicultural society   The effects of immigration in Dutch society are manifold and complex. In line with the Dutch liberal, tolerant society, all people are free to live the way they want. Dutch education facilitates foreign children to learn their parents' language and religion, many ethnic organisations are subsidised, foreigners have freedom of press and politics like any other citizen, and so forth.

'*Generally speaking, there is an atmosphere here of tolerance, equality and equal rights. In other so-called developed countries the locals act as if they're superior and they behave dominantly. Of course here too there are some people that act strange and discriminate in subtle ways, but the majority is tolerant and hospitable to foreigners.*' (Cambodia)

But not all is peace and quiet, neither among the native Dutch nor among the immigrant groups themselves. The so-called multicultural society is not developing without debate.

The aspect possibly appreciated the most is the availability of food and products from all over the world. Today, in cities all over the Netherlands one finds restaurants with 'exotic' cuisines ranging from by now traditional Chinese to more recent Thai or even Ethiopian. Shops sell hitherto unknown (sub)tropical fruits and vegetables, Islamic butchers offer good lamb, Turkish bakers produce good bread, Vietnamese market stalls fry fresh spring rolls, etc. Although many such shops cater for their own group, the Dutch gradually discover their delicacies as well. The Dutch dictum at the top of this chapter is fast eroding!

Quite a few people – especially among the better educated and the left-wing – plead for a multicultural society, colourful and tolerant. It should allow room for everyone to keep their identity and culture and yet mix with all other groups, enjoying each others' food, music, ceremonies and parties. Multicultural festivals are organised, people are invited to come and join in, and many do.

Yet, like in Dutch society itself, many people from the ethnic groups choose to live their life within their own group, not mixing much with the others. Among Dutch and non-Dutch citizens alike, stereotypes and prejudices about each other's culture are readily nurtured by doing so. Religious customs, class differences and living in this area rather than that also keep people separate. Ethnic dividing lines can easily evoke attitudes of 'us' and 'them' in spite of campaigns on TV and street posters to overcome such feelings.

'People from Turkey or Morocco can only marginally participate, not in leading positions or in politics. Within Dutch organisations foreigners get very few chances. People still think: if they can't speak Dutch exactly like us, their knowledge will probably be less also.' (Turkish business woman)

Sorrows   Dutch society, like others, has become much more complex in recent years. There is more potential for social circumstances to deteriorate into lawlessness. With increasing individualism and pluralism, disintegration of the social fabric can turn tolerance towards other groups into indifference.

Persistent unemployment and an outcast position may tempt youngsters (of all ethnicities, including the Dutch!) into illegal acts ranging from demolition to drug dealing and violent crime, causing irritation, fear and outrage among the victims and the general public. Reports and rumours of violence, theft, drug abuse, etc. do not appease the general feeling that society is heading for hard times. Outright racist groups, blaming 'the foreigners' for all social mishap, have arisen and even gained some political influence in places. Authorities are often not sure what to do about them. The liberal attitudes, which have been successful so far, are coming under pressure. It will take everyone's involvement and discipline to prevent ugly incidents. So far, little ethnic violence has taken place in the Netherlands. The Dutch solution to problems has always been: talk it over. Hopefully it will remain that way.

'Dutchmen pretend to be the conscience of the world. But you only need look about you or read the newspapers and you see a whole lot of discrimination. Here too, people are not treated equally. I was shocked to find they have a special word for everyone not born here.' (South Africa)

Only time will tell what the final outcome will be – if such a thing exists. Second and third generation immigrants blend in much more successfully than their parents. Mixed marriages occur increasingly, people meet in work places, schools and shops, during sports and other organisations. The government tries to decrease concentrations of certain ethnicities in particular areas. 'Ghetto formation', as it is called, must be avoided. After stressing 'positive discrimination' for some time, there are expectations that individual performance should do the trick.

'On the streets the Dutch make an incredibly tolerant impression: you see Chinese, Surinamese and Dutch people sitting in front of their houses. Nowhere in Europe, except maybe in Britain, will you find that. But if you talk to them, many frustrations surface. Their protests have been bought away by social securities. They have housing, food and that's how you keep them quiet.' (Germany)

All such measures cost money, and only general prosperity ensures social peace. Unless economic disaster occurs, there is a fair chance that in some decades people with Turkish or Moroccan family names will be just as unnoticed in Dutch society as French or German names are now, that Asian or African features will become as 'socially invisible' as people of Indonesian origin are now.

1. 1.1.1996; Statistics in this chapter from: CBS, *Statistisch Jaarboek 1997*, and Bohn, Stafleu, Van Lochum, *Jaarboek Minderheden 1997*.

Chapter 11

ON DO'S AND DON'TS

For those who just picked up this book without reading it yet,
and for readers as a summary up of the advice given
here and there in the book, we list some important
do's and don'ts in the Dutch business world.
This is what to expect in the *average situation* – but you
have to assess this for yourself!

Do's

When working or doing business with the Dutch:

- do come well-prepared, with detailed and practical information on your products/needs/capacities;
- do try to appear punctual, modest and practical;
- do try to give a positive but realistic, not 'overdone' presentation of your person, product or company;
- do seriously concentrate on the matter itself, with only occasional small talk or jokes until the business is over;
- do state your opinions clearly;
- do consult your Dutch colleagues at all levels (and don't take too long!);
- be prepared for criticism and for dealing calmly with it;
- be critical and outspoken on the Dutch, too; they expect and appreciate it;
- be open to compromise during any type of negotiations;
- do take initiatives and don't fear to lose face by being creative;
- do ask Dutch colleagues their opinion on your performance. Be prepared for very honest answers!
- do tell Dutch colleagues your views on the working environment and ways of doing somethings: 'constructive criticism' will be appreciated;
- do participate in small ceremonies like birthday coffee + cake, Sinterklaas or Christmas celebrations, etc.
- do try to learn (and practise) Dutch, even when everyone speaks English to you;
- do read and ask about Dutch history and society, you will understand the Dutch better.

Don'ts

- don't bring (or expect) expensive business presents;
- don't pride yourself on academic degrees, family relations, relations with important people during the introduction;
- don't overdress (look around you or ask Dutch advice);
- don't ask personal questions on income, political views, private life arrangements; at least not at the first meeting
- don't expect lavish meals or sightseeing trips in town. If you are offered them, it is obviously a good sign;
- don't expect intensive personal coaching outside work hours by the host company;
- don't expect the Dutch to come for a drink after work, but *do* ask again and again: one day they will come;
- when selling, don't forget to mention any price and environmental advantages of your product!
- don't expect (let alone ask) personal favours outside the transaction;
- don't over-compliment the Dutch;
- try to keep business and emotions somewhat separated during working hours;
- don't start long talks on philosophy, literature, art, etc. during introductions, business lunches, work hours, etc;
- when working with Dutch people: don't be bossy to any subordinates, ask them their opinion; after some time be a bit open about your personal background.

And now for the paradoxical questions from chapter 1:

1 *How do these 'money-minded people' accept such heavy taxes?*
They know that, generally, their precious tax money is not wasted but usefully employed for their own needs and those of less privileged sections of the population. See chapter 4.

2 *How can pornography be associated with wooden shoe wearing flower growers?*
It cannot. Both phenomena exist but are sensationally over-exploited in tourist propaganda, only vaguely reflecting two widely separate sections of Holland's pluriformous society, with very little contact in real life. See chapter 6.

3 *Where do the nice old gables fit in with the 'legal' drugs?*
Both exist, and both attract tourism, albeit from different 'target groups'. The drugs are not legal. See chapter 5.

4 *How can an industrial nation successfully compete on an image of cheese and windmills?*
Can it? Holland's industry and service sector deeply penetrate the world market, but with a rather low profile. The innocent windmill image is Holland's best known worldwide cliché, dating from earlier centuries, so even modern industry makes use of it.

5 *Why do people living in the constant danger of floods even bother with euthanasia?*
That 'constant danger' is hardly felt by the Dutch, who consider themselves in all-but-full control of their land. The Dutch euthanasia policy reflects the nation's practical attitude to life and death, and its concern for anyone suffering. See chapter 5.

6 *How come these football hooligans are so anti-German, being born about 30 years after the Second World War?*
This takes a somewhat longer answer. The Nazi occupation brought great misery to the Dutch, who were used to a quiet and non-violent society. It gave people perhaps the greatest (and longest lasting) shock of their lives, traumatising many, and they pass this on to their children and grand-children. Furthermore, even a small country needs a 'mental enemy', and the nearest large country comes in nicely then, especially since Germany is of course an economic giant as well. But the situation is improving, with Germany having greatly changed and Dutch media and education stressing that it is time to perceive Germany as it is now. See chapter 10.

Of course, many more paradoxes exist. I hope that most of these can be solved by reading this book. But there will always remain paradoxes that rational thinking cannot explain. I wish all readers a pleasant stay in the Netherlands, and satisfactory business opportunities and encounters.
As we say in Dutch: *Goede zaken!*

THE NETHERLANDS: AN OVERVIEW

General   The Netherlands lies in northwestern Europe, bordering on Germany and Belgium and facing Great Britain across the North Sea. It is quite small in size, only 120 km from the beach to the closest border and stretching a mere 400 km maximally. Area: 41,865 km² (15,770 sq. miles), including Waddenzee and IJsselmeer; land area: 33,800 km² .

Climate   The temperate maritime climate has winters with day temperatures around the freezing point, often with strong winds. Snow and severe frost occur in rare severe winters. Summers can be hot and sunny (30+°C in the daytime, and occasionally 20°C at night), but may also disappoint with much cooler, cloudy weather. Rain and humid air can occur in all seasons, making winter days chilly and summer days sticky. The Dutch weather is changeable and unpredictable, which might explain its importance as a topic of casual conversation.

Scenery   The country is flat, with man-made land ('reclaimed' lakes and swamps) lying under sea level *(polders)*. This is generally true for the northern and western half, where water is to be seen almost everywhere: rivers, canals, lakes, estuaries and the omnipresent ditches that drain the low grasslands, giving them a carved-up and neat appearance. The lowest point, near Rotterdam, is some -7 meters (-23 feet).

The east and south of the country are slightly higher and drier. There you can find some sandy elevations, forest and heather areas, and in some places hills of more than 100 meters. In the extreme southeast, in Limburg province, the hills reach the national maximum of +321 meters (1053 feet). Although the country is densely populated, strict control on building safeguards open spaces that come across as green and clean and quite charming to foreign eyes.

Natural resources   The main assets of the Dutch economy have always been its fertile land and its favourable location on the rivers and seas of Western Europe, stimulating trade.

Subterranean Holland was always regarded as quite poor in minerals. Up to the 1970s coal was produced in quantities that did not allow export, there was small-scale exploitation of oil and iron ore, and of clay and gravel for construction. But in 1960, enormous quantities of natural gas, plus some more oil, were discovered, in the north of the country and in the Dutch part of the North Sea.

Economy   No doubt related to its green appearance, Holland has a strongly agricultural image abroad. However, by no means do milk, cheese and flower bulbs represent a realistic picture. The agro-industry is much more varied than that, with an export value second only to that of the USA. Just over 2% of all working people are employed in agriculture itself, reflecting its high mechanisation and automation.

The Dutch economy is predominantly industrial and service-oriented, with a strongly international orientation based on its long trading tradition and colonial past. A disproportionally high number of trans-national companies reflect this. Companies like Ahold, Akzo-Nobel, DSM, Philips, Shell, Stork, Unilever, Wolters-Kluwer/Reed-Elsevier, and financial organisations like ABN/Amro, Aegon, ING, KPN and Rabo are well-known abroad, but not always identified as totally or partly Dutch.

Oil industry, machinery, electronics and other high-tech production and a large and varied agro-industry are responsible for the bulk of the economic output, together with transport and other trade-related facilities like banking and insurance.

The carefully managed exploitation and export of Holland's large reserves of natural gas has given a sound basis to the Dutch economy ever since the early 1960s, producing one of the world's strongest currencies, the guilder.

Activities such as (incoming) tourism and the breeding of oysters and mussels for foreign markets are eye-catching but in fact marginal when compared with the size of more conventional activities. Few people realize that the banknotes of many countries are printed in the Nether-lands, that their CD's may have been produced in Holland, their booming ports reconstructed by specialised Dutch building companies, their ships-in-trouble saved by Dutch maritime services. They may enjoy Dutch ice cream, cook with Holland-produced dried spices and, indeed, feed their babies on Dutch milk powder, have Dutch flowers in their vases, look at a Dutch-printed poster on the wall.

On a more abstract – and culture-related – level the Dutch economy can be described as a mixture of free market economy and fairly strong government control. A deeply felt need to have everyone share a decent level of living has led to a system in which national wealth is distributed to all, to some extent.

Another aspect of state control is the regulations that enterprise has to follow: safety and hygiene, salary levels, workers' rights, environmental restrictions, all kinds of limitations on building, and many others.

Yet Holland has much to offer to foreign investors: a highly educated working force; an excellent coastal position in the heart of the world's largest trading block; nearby emerging markets; very good infrastructure; and, in spite of the otherwise high taxation, favourable tax rates for foreign investment.

Spread of population   With close on 16 million inhabitants the Netherlands is the world's fourth most densely populated country (after Bangladesh, Taiwan and South Korea). The spread of the population, and therefore of economic activities, is very uneven. The emptier areas are to be found in the northeast and the southwest. Nearly half the national population lives in the west, in the so-called Randstad.

Language   Dutch, a Germanic language like German and English, is spoken throughout the country, with various regional dialects. Friesland province, in the north, has its own language, related to Dutch.
Many of the Dutch speak English, but it is not always fluent.

Religion   Since the 1500s Calvinism, a rather strict Protestant denomination, dominated the region north of the rivers dividing the Netherlands in the middle, while in the south the great majority remained Catholic. Nowadays, only some 25% of the Dutch regularly attend church services. Among the ethnic minorities Islam is the most widespread religion.

Education   Education in Holland, organised in the continental European tradition, is good according to international standards, albeit with little mixture of theory and practice. Both state and private schools are government-funded and therefore free or nearly free up to age 16. After that age, an extensive state scholarship system helps people to partly finance further studies, regardless of parental income.

State control results in fairly even quality throughout the country, including the universities, although some faculties may enjoy a particularly good reputation. For jobs in the business world, MBA studies and HEAO (a subacademic training) are widely popular nowadays.

School attendance is obligatory up to age 16, and remains high afterwards. Some 7% of the population has completed academic education.

For foreigners, there are some schools with a British, American or Japanese curriculum.

Basic history

40 BC - 4th century AD - Areas south of the river Rhine are part of the Roman Empire. To the north are tribal areas.

5th - 8th century - The southern part of the Netherlands is part of the Frankish, Merovingian and Carolingian empires.

8th - 10th century - Charlemagne conquers the Frisians; from 870 the Low Countries (including Belgium and Luxembourg) form part of the East Frankish Empire, and from 962, the Holy Roman Empire.

10th - 11th century - Feudalism reigns.

12th and 13th century - As the population grows, low-lying marshlands in the west come under cultivation. Peasants and fishermen build dykes to protect their property and lives, creating 'waterschappen', organisations for the construction, maintenance and repair of dykes and sluices; many of the Dutch provinces were first established in these centuries.

15th and 16th century - Through inheritance, the Low Countries become part of the Burgundian empire, later of Habsburg Spain. Hanseatic cities develop maritime trade with West European lands.

16th century - Reformation gains many followers in the Low Countries. Reacting to oppression by Catholic Spain, the Protestants rise up and declare independence in 1581: the Republic of the Seven United Nether-lands, a federation of seven northern provinces with Holland province in control. The Princes of Orange-Nassau are in power but not royal. The Calvinist religion comes to dominate, Catholics have to go into hiding. The revolt is won around 1590, but formally lasts until 1648. The south remains Catholic, partly occupied by the Dutch Republic, partly Spanish (Belgium).

17th century - Pursuing the Spanish enemy and its ally Portugal, the Dutch Republic develops a highly successful and worldwide maritime trade empire, focusing on the East Indian Archipelago, present day Indonesia. The republic enters its Golden Age, with prosperity for many, city build-ing, flourishing art, vast land reclamations and international prestige. Gradually, a national identity develops.

18th century - Stagnation of Holland's maritime trade in the face of British competition.

1795-1813 - Anti-Orangist regime based on French revolutionary prin-ciples, followed by French occupation. Napoleon's brother Louis becomes the first king of this vassal state (1806). Catholicism becomes accepted once again.

1813 - Restoration of independence, reunited with Belgium. The Prince of Orange becomes King. Belgium industrialises, the north remains mostly agrarian. North-south antagonisms increase. The word 'Netherlands' is used more often. Belgium separates in 1830.

1880 - After a period of stagnation, the Dutch economy starts industrialising and modernising. In Indonesia, colonial rule and exploitation are intensified, bringing the Netherlands great profit. Various religious and political groups set up their own political parties, organisations and education systems, leading to social compartmentalisation.

1914-1918 - The Netherlands remains neutral in World War I. The 1916 floods lead to the closing off and reclaiming of the Zuiderzee.

1920s - Modest prosperity, increasing industrialisation and modernisation. Radio is introduced, organised into separate socio-religious broadcasting organisations.

1930s - Severe economic crisis, government increases its grip on the economy in an attempt to solve massive unemployment.

1940 - 1945 - Nazi occupation, 100,000 Dutch Jews killed in concentration camps, another 100,000 people in acts of war and repression. Enormous economic damage ensues. In the face of fighting the enemy, social compartmentalisation is temporarily overcome.

1945 - Liberation by Allied armies. After Japan's occupation of the Dutch East Indies, Indonesia declares independence. Dutch forces unsuccessfully try to suppress this for 4 years. Colonial functionaries and the military, including some Indonesian citizens, are expelled by Indonesia.

1950s - With US aid ('Marshall-aid'), the Netherlands slowly recovers its prosperity. Hard work, savings and obedience to leadership are emphasised. The 1953 flood in the southwest, killing 1850 people, leads to the Delta project, closing out the sea from between the islands.

1960s - Beginning of the welfare state, made possible also by the discovery and exploitation of large quantities of natural gas. Student protest against authoritarian education system leads to a youth revolt and vast social changes after 1965, resulting in more democratic relations and loosening of religious bonds. Gradually, the social compartmentalisation starts breaking up.

1970s - More prosperous than ever before. Under strong social-democratic influence, social benefits and taxes grow to the highest levels in the world. Labour immigration from Turkey and Morocco, and people from former Caribbean colonies create ethnic minorities.

1980s - Under liberal/Christian-democratic government prosperity continues but does not grow. Economic recession, growing unemployment and persistent state budget deficit. Attempts at economising on welfare and other state expenses. Some ethnic tensions emerge in the cities.

1990s - Economy recovers with ups and downs. The 1994 liberal/social-democratic government stimulates self-employment and further 'deregulation'. This leads to the creation of many jobs and to economic growth higher than in surrounding countries. Large infrastructural works are under way: cargo railroad Rotterdam-Germany, high speed trains, further expansion of Schiphol Airport.

INDEX